The
TWELVE LESSON COURSE

In

A NEW APPROACH TO VIOLIN PLAYING

By

KATÓ HAVAS

With exercises relating to
the fundamental balances

Bosworth

To David Mendoza for those wonderful lessons in New York so many years ago when much of the 'New Approach' was born, and to the memory of Imre Waldbauer, the founder of many of the balances in this book, for an unforgettable musical childhood in Budapest.

10th Impression 2003

CONTENTS

INTRODUCTION

In my book "A New Approach to Violin Playing", I tried to explain that the technique I am expounding "is not to be regarded as some sudden mushroom discovery, totally new and revolutionary, in the sense of a patent medicine. Many of the most important elements are derived from the teachings of the great masters of the past, to whom I pay glad and grateful homage. What I do claim is that these elements have been, through slow experience, integrated into a new form, a working system that may well have been touched upon accidentally and in part by others before me, but has not, to my knowledge, ever been formulated before."

The wide interest in that little book and the enthusiasm of the many teachers and players who came in contact with this Approach made it necessary for me to continue with more detailed explanations.

I must add that although many of the most important elements of this Approach *are* derived from the teachings of great masters, the difference between this and the conventional methods begins in the very foundations. So in order to try and convey a thorough understanding, I have decided to set down a series of twelve lessons from the beginning, with the appropriate exercises. These lessons are meant to be approximately of an hour's duration. But of course, each player should advance at his own speed. One lesson may take two hours; another may take half. There certainly should not be any hard and fast rules.

Also I would like to emphasise that these lessons are not meant for beginners alone. They are very similar to the courses I give to every player who comes to me, regardless of whether he is a well-known violinist, an unknown teacher, or, for that matter any kind of amateur or beginner. The joys and heart-aches of violin playing are common to all players alike. As far as the basic problems are concerned, the division between a beginner or a virtuoso is much smaller than one would imagine. Of course, with an advanced player the lessons would be focused on his individual problem and the approach is adapted to suit his particular physique and mentality, but to eliminate that problem, a thorough understanding of every step from the beginning is indispensible.

However, keeping in mind the beginners, I have tried to set a slow enough pace with adequate exercises to make them feel as relaxed as possible while they are working on this book. I have as a matter of course, assumed some knowledge of theory.

Although I shall often repeat instructions in order to emphasise a point more strongly I must emphasize too that no one, at least in the early stages, can possibly hope to learn the violin without a teacher. What is more, this book is not meant to be read at a single sitting. Although it is true that when this Approach has been assimilated violin playing is made far easier, the assimilation itself may not be easy at all.

I cannot therefore emphasize too strongly that the reader of this book (regardless of whether he is a beginner or an advanced player) must not go from one lesson to the next, or indeed from one point to the next until each idea (*and the logic behind it*) has been completely understood—and tried. It is very important that the beginner should never do anything simply because he is told to do so. Questions and discussions should be encouraged by the teacher.

Another important thing is that beginners should not practise on their own between lessons, until they reach the end of this book. They should do only the *silent* or singing exercises outlined after each lesson.

I hope that in this way the book will prove to be a help both to the player and to the teacher, for as I pointed out in my other book, the aim is to eliminate both physical and mental obstacles so that through a relaxed and controlled co-ordination, the player may be able to release the full force of his musical imagination.

LESSON I

THE APPROACH TO VIOLIN PLAYING

"Those who understand the peculiar relation of the performing artist and connoisseur to his string instrument" writes Karel Jalovec in his 'ITALIAN VIOLIN MAKERS' "must learn to regard the violin and its larger relatives as works of art. The feelings of part and partiality, of extreme fondness and love that certain instruments evoke, even of regret, when some quality is lacking or destroyed, can be understood only if this artistic approach is used."

This idea that the violin is a work of art should be clear to every beginner. By work of art one does not necessarily mean a Stradivarius or Guarnarius etc. By work of art one simply means that each violin by its very nature is an object of beauty and should be appreciated as such. The beginner should be fully aware even before touching the instrument, what a tremendous privilege it is to have works of art as tools for making music. But he should be even more aware that this privilege involves great responsibilities too. As Kreisler has said "it is the player that produces the tone, not the violin."

If a violin is properly played its tone closely resembles singing. And singing is as old as man and as fundamental as life : it is the most natural and most spontaneous means of musical expression. And it is this aim of recapturing the quality of the human voice with all its warmth and expressiveness that demands such great artistic responsibility from anybody who plays the violin.

Almost as if to emphasise its close relationship with a living being, the various parts of the violin are named after the human body too.

Illustration 1

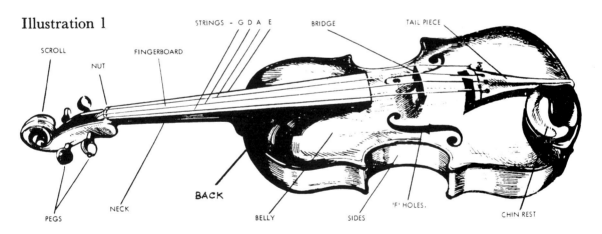

Because the violin reacts to changes in humidity and temperature it should be wrapped, when not in use, in a square piece of wool or flannel cloth. A duster should be kept in the case and all resin dust should be cleaned off the strings and body every time after it has been played. Each violin should be equipped with a chin-rest and shoulder-pad. (See A NEW APPROACH TO VIOLIN PLAYING, p.13).

THE FUNDAMENTAL BALANCES

The conventional conception that it is inevitable for a beginner to screech and gurgle on the violin, and to ache and suffer while playing it, is wrong. An ugly sound simply means that the violin is maltreated and that erroneous limb and muscle actions are used. On the other hand, the idea that violin playing (or for that matter, any kind of art), is easy, is not right either.

However it is most important to understand that the real difficulties are seldom caused by "technique" as the word is usually understood. The difficulties lie in the false notion that violin playing depends on the use of some sort of superimposed pressure or force. This mistaken idea inevitably results in faulty movements which in turn create an overall state of anxiety. And the awful thing about anxiety is that, at the slightest provocation, it can spread like wildfire, paralyzing the mind, crippling the body, until everything seems unduly difficult and all artistic expression becomes nothing but a monumental struggle. So the first and most important object for each beginner is to eradicate this faulty idea of having to use any force. Instead, good violin playing, as it will be seen, depends on the co-ordination of a host of delicate balances which in turn demand a high degree of mental discipline. This is what every player must learn from the very beginning: *where the fundamental balances concerning violin playing are and the control and co-ordination of them from the mind.*

Once this is achieved there is no earthly reason (as has been proved to me and to those who are teaching this approach), why a beginner should not have a singing tone from the very start. There is no such thing as one sort of tone production in the beginning and another sort later on. As far as I am concerned the idea of violin playing is similar to the idea of tight-rope walking. If one is to manage at all, the right balances must be controlled and co-ordinated from the very beginning, regardless of whether the rope is stretched near the ground or high in the air.

It is important to understand that the fundamental balances in violin playing are not always visible and that we must trace each action to its source. For example, each time the left arm is lifted into position for violin playing, the *source* of this movement is *behind* in the muscles which attach the shoulder-blade to the spine, though what we *see* is only the movement of the arm. But in fact without the motivation of these muscles in the shoulder-blade, the arm could not lift into position. So, tempting as it is to think about the action which we can see, that is, the movement of the arm, concentration should be focused on the source which causes it to move, that is, on the muscle behind the shoulder-blade.

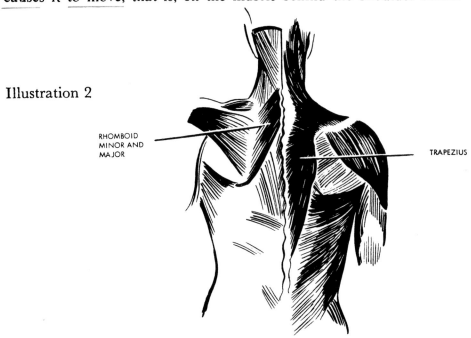

Illustration 2

RHOMBOID MINOR AND MAJOR

TRAPEZIUS

THE SEE-SAW IMAGE

The left arm position under the violin is unnatural as it is. Just think what torture it would be considered if one were told to keep one's arm raised like that for hours on end as a punishment; a rather unfavourable condition for spontaneous artistic impulses. Yet this is the position violinists are up against. So it cannot be underlined enough how vital it is to learn to concentrate on the right point of balance which is able not only to counterbalance the stress of this position, but, which by its fundamental power, can create a feeling of security as well.

The image of the see-saw will help to explain the idea of balance and counterbalance and how this can achieve greater power than mere force ever could.

Illustration 3

Imagine a very large and heavy plank which would require great strength to lift and which would be impossible to hold. Then imagine a pivot placed underneath it exactly in the middle. Both sides of the plank are suspended, even though the area of support is so small. Although the plank was so heavy before that one could hardly lift it, it is now so beautifully balanced that the slightest movement of the hand can set it in motion. And as most of us have see-sawed sometime or other in our lives, I hardly need to explain how an even movement depends entirely on an adjustment of weight and never *never* on force.

Good violin playing depends exactly on the same kind of balances. So I shall often use the see-saw image to help to illustrate the fundamental balances both great and small.

For example, as I have said before, the source of the left arm movement is in the big muscle in the back around the spine and the shoulder-blade (see illustration 2). So imagine that your body is the pivot and that your left arm forms one end of the see-saw. But as there is no arm in the back to counterbalance it, we must create a substitute, a *feeling* of weight hanging from the shoulder-blade. This feeling, this imaginary weight hanging from the shoulder-blade should be heavier than the arm so that, as on the see-saw, the arm, being the lighter end, can rise. And what we shall achieve is a feeling of suspension in the left arm. As the motivating power for the arm movement is in the back, in the muscles between the spine and the shoulder-blade anyhow, the feeling of weight hanging there should not be hard to imagine.

This see-saw image with the feeling of weight in the back will also apply to the right arm and will be a great help to all bowing technique.

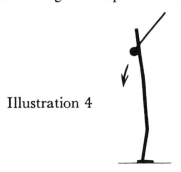

Illustration 4

THE STANCE

The mental image of the see-saw also has the effect of establishing a balanced stance which is invaluable in the elimination of anxiety. For the feeling of weight in the back prevents the body from bending forward and with the weight of the violin in the front becoming top-heavy. This feeling of weight in the back acts as a perfect counter-balance to the jutting forward position of the violin because it creates a sensation of 'tilting backwards' onto the heels and onto the bottom of the spine, as if leaning against a wall.

The same feeling can be obtained when playing in a sitting position; the "tilting backwards" is then simply on the bottom of the spine. (See A NEW APPROACH TO VIOLIN PLAYING, p.15).

There is an enormous difference between the two conceptions of *lifting* or *suspending* the arm. If the arm is merely lifted from the hand (as if playing the violin) it feels heavy and becomes tired in a very short time. On the other hand if it is raised from its socket on the principle of the see-saw action, the feeling of weight in the back provides the necessary support by which the arm remains suspended for long periods without any fatigue at all.

EXERCISE 1

SUSPEND THE LEFT ARM IN MID-AIR AS IF PLAYING THE VIOLIN BUT AT FIRST *WITHOUT* THE INSTRUMENT. REPEAT THIS MOVEMENT ABOUT TWELVE TIMES UNTIL THE DIFFERENCE BETWEEN *LIFTING* AND *SUSPENDING* IS QUITE CLEAR. IT WILL BE SEEN THAT THE MORE FEELING OF WEIGHT THERE IS BEHIND IN THE SHOULDER-BLADES, THE LIGHTER THE ARM WILL SEEM IN THE FRONT. AND A LIGHT ARM WHICH DOES NOT GET STIFF OR TIRED IS INDISPENSABLE TO GOOD VIOLIN PLAYING.

EXERCISE 2

NOW TRY THE SAME MOVEMENT WITH THE VIOLIN. THE AIM IS TO MAKE THE VIOLIN, TOO, FEEL AS WEIGHTLESS AS POSSIBLE.

HANG THE VIOLIN VERTICALLY FROM YOUR LEFT HAND. HOLD IT RIGHT UNDER THE PEGS BETWEEN THE FINGERS AND THUMB KEEPING THE ARM SLIGHTLY BENT.

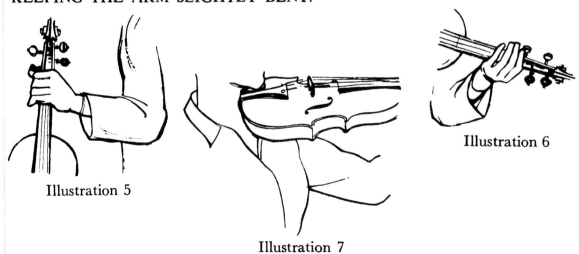

Illustration 5

Illustration 6

Illustration 7

THEN WITH A SWIFT ARM MOVEMENT (FROM THE SHOULDER-BLADE) AND A LIGHT TURN OF THE HAND TOWARDS THE LEFT, THE VIOLIN IS THROWN, OR RATHER, IS TOSSED ONTO THE COLLAR

BONE. THE SUCCESS OF ACHIEVING A FEATHER-WEIGHT-LIKE FEELING OF THE VIOLIN DEPENDS ON THE SWIFTNESS OF ARM AND HAND MOVEMENTS. THIS EXERCISE IS OF PARAMOUNT IMPORTANCE BECAUSE IT IS THE FIRST STEP TOWARDS MAKING THE PLAYER FEEL THAT *THE VIOLIN IS AN EXTENSION OF HIMSELF AND NOT A CUMBERSOME BURDEN.*

This swift tossing motion might seem somewhat difficult at the start. The tendency with many beginners will be to do it slowly at first because they may lack the necessary courage for the rapid movement. But of course the more slowly it is done, the heavier the violin seems, and the heavier the violin becomes, the more courage it takes to toss it. And so it becomes a vicious circle creating anxiety instead of eliminating it. If this is the case it is most important that the beginner does not force this action with hard, impatient movements. If it proves difficult the best possible thing is to put the violin down and simply *think* about the movement. And then when this process of tossing is quite clear in the mind, try again. Alternate this process of trying it and thinking about it and the result will be startlingly quick and good.

Much struggle and useless work could be avoided if the silent "thinking" practice were more developed. For no physical action can take place without an order from the mind. This is why mental discipline plays such a tremendously important role in good violin playing; for if the mind is disciplined to give orders only to those basic points which are the key positions of the fundamental balances, these fundamental balances in turn will have the power to motivate a chain of other actions as well.

The brain is rather like a puppet master manipulating his puppet theatre. At the pull of the key string the puppet will bow, smile, turn his head, and at the same time perhaps even put a hand on his heart. So a skilled puppet master, who knows how to control the strings, can create a whole play with only two hands.

THE VIOLIN HOLD

The fundamental balance in the actual violin hold is also in the back, though what we see is the jaw holding the violin in the front. However unless the head itself is lowered, there can be no contact between the jaw and the violin. And the source of this movement of lowering the head comes from behind, from the first vertebra under the skull. So it is really the forward motion caused by the weight from the back of the head that places the jaw and part of the chin on the chin-rest.

The violin itself is placed on the collar bone with the button at the end of the tail-piece pointing towards the hollow of the throat. The weight on the chin-rest from the back of the head creates not only a natural position, but also serves as a perfect counter-balance to the jutting forward position of the violin. It enables the main body of the violin to tilt upward by itself without the support of the left arm. The actual point of contact between lower jaw and chin-rest depends on the build of each individual and on the type of chin-rest used.

(See DRAWINGS 3 and 4 in A NEW APPROACH TO VIOLIN PLAYING, p.17).

EXERCISE 3

TRY THIS MOVEMENT FIRST WITHOUT THE VIOLIN. THROW THE HEAD BACKWARDS AND THEN DROP IT FORWARD WITH A SWIFT RELAXED MOVEMENT. IT IS A SIMPLE STRAIGHTFORWARD ACTION WHICH ENABLES THE JAW TO DROP ONTO THE COLLAR

BONE. BUT BE CAREFUL THAT IT IS THE *BACK* OF THE HEAD THAT IS THROWN FORWARD. *DO NOT STRETCH THE NECK.* REPEAT THIS SIX TIMES. THEN PLACE THE VIOLIN ON THE COLLAR BONE WITH THE END OF THE TAILPIECE POINTING INTO THE HOLLOW OF THE THROAT. THROW THE HEAD BACK AS BEFORE AND THEN DROP IT FORWARD ONTO THE CHIN-REST. DO THIS ABOUT TWELVE TIMES UNTIL ALL TENDENCY OF STRAIN AND STRESS IS REMOVED FROM THE NECK AND THE SIDE OF THE JAW. WHEN THIS IS ACHIEVED, LET THE LEFT ARM HANG FOR A SECOND BY THE SIDE OF THE BODY. DO NOT LET YOUR NECK AND JAW MUSCLES TIGHTEN ON THE CHIN-REST WHILE YOU DO THIS, BUT THINK OF THE WEIGHT OF THE BACK OF THE HEAD DOING THE WORK. THIS CAN *NOT* BECOME TIGHT. REST A SHORT WHILE AND THEN TRY THE EXERCISE AGAIN, BUT LEAVE THE LEFT ARM HANGING FOR A LONGER TIME. REPEAT THIS SIX TIMES, THEN REST, THEN SIX TIMES AGAIN LEAVING THE LEFT ARM HANGING BY THE SIDE OF THE BODY LONGER AND LONGER EACH TIME.

Please do not go about it with too much physical determination and force, because that is what causes stress and strain. Rest frequently between doing the exercises and *think* about the movement. Make it clear to yourself over and over again that holding the violin is not a matter of physical endurance but a question of finding the right *balance*.

Those beginners to whom holding the violin does not come easily, achieve much better results if they put the violin away completely for long periods. They should *imagine* how it would feel to hold it so lightly and easily, (without the support of the left arm) that they could sing an aria and dance a Pas de Deux without even noticing that the violin is attached to them. Learning to hold the violin is rather like learning to ride a bicycle : once the balance is found, nothing could be easier, but until the balance *is* found—no amount of physical force will help.

Illustration 8

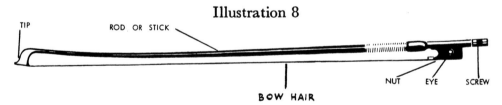

THE BOW-HOLD

The bow-hold, just like the violin hold, is created by a feeling of balance. This is an essential fact to understand even before touching the bow. For as soon as the slightest force is used, it stiffens the fingers and the wrist and as a result the bowing arm may be ruined for life. But once a feeling of balance is achieved, no force will ever be necessary.

As no two hands are the same, the bow-hold must vary with each individual. It would be a great mistake to be categorical about it. To find out what suits each player best, one has simply to follow what nature has intended. For example if you hang your right arm by the side of your body, you will see that the tendency of the fingers and thumb is to curve slightly inward towards the palm. If you lift the fore-arm (not the whole arm, only the fore-arm) with the fingers curved in the same position as when the arm was hanging, you will see that the tip of the thumb tends to point somewhere between the 1st and 2nd fingers.

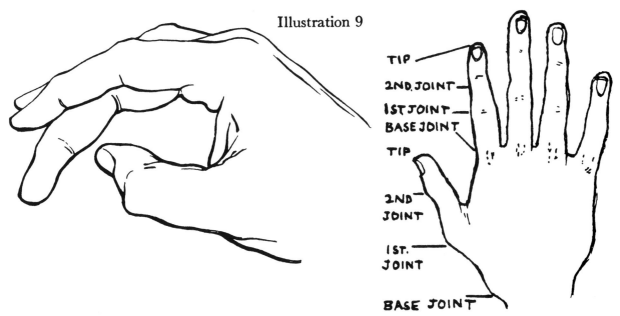

Illustration 9

TIP — 2ND JOINT — 1ST JOINT — BASE JOINT — TIP — 2ND JOINT — 1ST. JOINT — BASE JOINT

In some cases the curve will be more towards the index finger, in others, towards the middle finger. But whichever way the thumb tends to bend by nature, that is the position of the bow-hold which most probably suits you best. Make certain, however, that while you are trying this the wrist is so loose that even the lightest breeze could flutter it, as if it were no heavier than a leaf. If this proves difficult, hang your arm again by your side and shake it lightly to dispel all tension, then try the bow-hold again with the fore-arm lifted as before.

Now when it actually comes to holding the bow, there is a tendency, because of its weight, to 'clutch' the stick. One must anticipate and prevent this. So take the bow in your *left* hand first, and hold it at the screw between the thumb and the index finger with the hair facing up and at right angles to your body. Tilt the tip of the bow slightly upwards pointing to the right. This way you will be able to *see* what the right hand has to do and there will be no tendency to clutch.

While still holding the bow in the left hand with the hair facing you, place the outside of the extreme edge of the right thumb-tip (i.e. the farthest side from the hand) against the edge of the protruding part of the nut between the hair and the stick. The thumb itself is bent *outward*, especially the 2nd joint, so that the area below the nail rests against the point where the hair joins the nut. After the thumb-tip is established at the edge of the nut, it is the middle part of the middle finger between the first and second joints that is placed on the stick. Put down the bow, hang your arm by the side of your body and try out the natural position of your hand again. Note carefully where the middle part of the middle finger is in relation to the tip of the thumb. Wherever it goes, it should be approximately in the same position, relative to the thumb, when it is placed on the stick.

The circle between the tip of the thumb and the middle part of the middle finger is the pivot of the bow-hold. The index finger acts as one end of the balance and the little finger as the other end. (Illustration 9).

The middle finger is placed *slant-wise* on the stick. It embraces the stick, so that the end of the finger is in the direction of the 'eye' of the nut. From the point of view of balance *this slanting position is most necessary because it ensures that the fore-arm and hand are turned inward toward the violin* (when the bow is on the strings), *which in turn ensures that it is the side of the index finger that rests on the stick, while the little finger falls on its tip.* If all these positions are correct the 3rd finger will take its place naturally according to the size and shape of the hand. The side of the index-finger should rest somewhere between the 1st and 2nd joints and should never be allowed to slide beyond the first. This is very important as otherwise the feeling of balance is lost, and the muscle under the index finger becomes stiff.

Conceive the image of the see-saw again, this time in a miniature form, and it will be seen how inevitable it is for the thumb at one side of the stick (bent outward) and the middle part of the middle finger on the other side (placed slant-wise) to act as the pivot around which the side of the index finger (between the 1st and 2nd joints) and the little finger (on its tip) balance the weight of the bow, depending on whether the stroke begins at the nut or at the tip.

Now tilt the stick upright, so that it is vertical, and hold it with the right hand alone in *exactly* the same position. The muscle under the thumb should stay completely relaxed. Then, finally, tilt the stick towards the left into the actual position of playing. Rest the hair on the back of the left hand, this time to avoid the pull on the little finger in the right hand which the weight of the bow may cause.

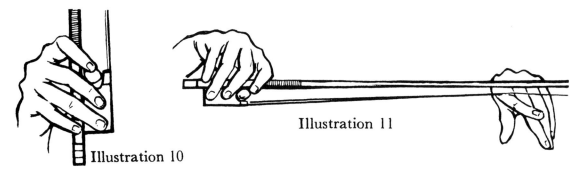

Illustration 11

Illustration 10

EXERCISE 4

TRY THE BOW-HOLD OVER AND OVER AGAIN *WITHOUT HOLD-ING THE BOW AT FIRST*. MAKE CERTAIN THAT THERE IS A CIRCLE BETWEEN THE TIP OF THE THUMB AND THE MIDDLE PART OF THE MIDDLE FINGER, (THIS IS THE BOW-HOLD WHICH SUITS MOST PEOPLE BEST; THAT IS WHY I AM USING IT AS AN EXAMPLE) AND THAT YOUR ARM AND FORE-ARM ARE TURNED TO THE LEFT SO THAT THE PALM OF YOUR HAND IS TURNED TO THE RIGHT, AWAY FROM YOUR BODY. ALTERNATE THIS OCCASIONALLY BY HANGING YOUR ARM AT THE SIDE OF YOUR BODY. THEN SHAKE THE ARM AND WRIST LIGHTLY TO MAKE CERTAIN THEY REMAIN LOOSE.

EXERCISE 5

HOLD THE BOW IN YOUR LEFT HAND AT RIGHT ANGLES TO YOUR BODY, AS DESCRIBED BEFORE AND ONLY THEN TRY THE BOW-HOLD WITH THE RIGHT HAND. MAKE CERTAIN THAT THE RIGHT WRIST AND FINGERS REMAIN COMPLETELY LOOSE. THEN TILT THE STICK UPRIGHT IN A VERTICAL POSITION AND HOLD IT ONLY IN THE RIGHT HAND, THE FINGERS REMAINING AS LIGHT AS BEFORE. THIS EXERCISE SHOULD BE REPEATED OVER AND OVER AGAIN UNTIL THE BEGINNER ACHIEVES COMPLETE ASSURANCE, AND THE BOW IS LIGHT ENOUGH TO SEEM A MERE EXTENSION OF THE HAND. ONLY THEN TILT THE STICK TOWARDS THE LEFT INTO THE ACTUAL POSITION OF PLAYING, RESTING THE HAIR ON THE BACK OF THE LEFT HAND.

IT IS VERY IMPORTANT NOT TO RUSH THIS EXERCISE, BECAUSE ALL FUTURE DEXTERITY DEPENDS ON THE FEELING OF THIS LIGHT AND EASY BALANCE. PATIENCE AND THOROUGH UNDERSTANDING IN THE BEGINNING WILL BE MORE THAN REWARDED LATER.

READ OVER AND *THINK* ABOUT ALL THESE POINTS BUT DO NOT ACTUALLY TRY TO HOLD THE VIOLIN AND BOW UNTIL YOUR NEXT LESSON.

NOTE TO THE ADVANCED PLAYER

The previous exercises may seem deceptively elementary to the advanced player. But in order to understand this Approach fully one must realise the enormous difference that lies between the 'elementary' and the 'fundamental'; and it is needless to say that nothing could be more fundamental than establishing an effortless balance of the violin- and bow-holds.

The advanced player tends to take the correctness of his violin- and bow-holds far too much for granted. However, if his jaw is sore or red he can be certain that he is gripping the violin (see A New Approach to Violin Playing, page 8), and if there are callouses on his right thumb and index finger he can be certain that he is gripping the bow. Often have I traced the cause of the difficulty of many a violinist, who came to me for help (with seemingly different problems), to a conscious or subconscious anxiety about the violin- or bow-hold.

LESSON II

THE BOW-STROKE

Before going any further, think over the see-saw image, the principle of the stance (p. 3,4). The violin-hold, (p.5), and the bow-hold (p.6). Then repeat Exercises 1 (p.4), 2 (p.4), 3 (p. 5), 4 (p. 8). 5 (p. 8).

Now although a correct bow-hold is essential, it is vital to understand that the fundamental balance which *motivates* the bow-stroke and all bowing technique as well, is in the rear, hidden in the intricate mechanism of the shoulder-blade. For as was explained before, it is here, in the muscles which attach the shoulder-blade to the spine, that the source of the arm movement originates. Because of the erroneous conception of following only what one *sees*, i.e. the up and down movements of the fore-arm, people are apt to think it is the fore-arm that controls the bow-stroke. But as the fore-arm is *not* the source of movement, it can not, in fact, control anything. And if it tries, if it tries to control something it *cannot* control, it merely creates a state of anxiety which is very difficult to overcome. As a result of this, the wrist and bow-hold become stiff, the movements awkward and one of the greatest stumbling blocks in violin playing is created. And once this is allowed to happen, none of the countless 'wrist' or 'finger' exercises will help.

So it is absolutely essential (as it was with the left arm) to understand and to give due importance to the motivating balance. For this in turn can control and co-ordinate the *whole* bowing arm including the fore-arm, wrist and fingers. Indeed one has only to watch a baby taking his first steps to realize the significance of the motivating balances. At first his steps are straight from the hips where the leg movement originates. And only afterwards do his knees and ankles become flexible as a result of the basic balance which is able to co-ordinate the rest. The realization of this principle will eliminate much struggle and unnecessary practice.

The see-saw image will be a great help again. Imagine (as with the violin-hold before) that your body is the pivot and that your right arm *with the bow* is the light end, while the heavy end is the imaginary weight in the back, hanging from your shoulder-blade. And because of this imaginary weight in the back, the right arm will feel suspended, as did the left. As a result of this, the fore-arm, wrist and hand, *including the bow*, will seem weightless, and the bow-stroke will become a floating action instead of a physical effort.

X X **EXERCISE 6**
SIDEWAYS

DROP YOUR RIGHT ARM DOWN BESIDE YOUR BODY. BEND IT AT THE ELBOW; THEN RAISE THE UPPER-ARM SLIGHTLY UNTIL YOUR WRIST (PALM DOWNWARDS) IS LEVEL WITH YOUR SHOULDER. IMAGINE, ON THE PRINCIPLE OF THE SEE-SAW, THAT THE WEIGHT IN THE BACK IS HEAVY ENOUGH SO THAT THE ARM (ESPECIALLY THE FORE-ARM AND HAND) HAS NO ALTERNATIVE BUT TO RISE IN THE FRONT. REPEAT THIS MOVEMENT OVER AND OVER AGAIN WITHOUT HOLDING THE BOW, UNTIL THE FEELING OF THE 'FLOATING' FORE-ARM AND HAND IS WELL ESTABLISHED.

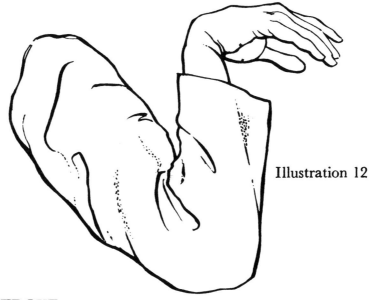

Illustration 12

THE DOWN-STROKE

In order to understand the nature of the strokes, let us take the idea of the see-saw a step further. Relying on the support of the imaginary heavy weight in the back where the motivating force originates, imagine that the suspended light end in the front is on a spring which opens and shuts like a concertina.

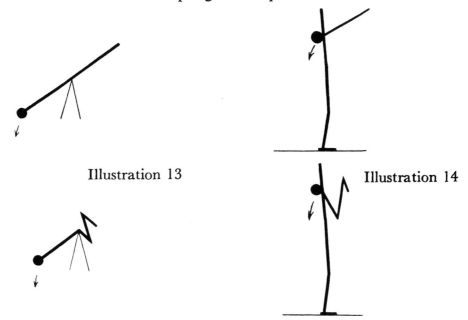

Illustration 13   Illustration 14

It is most important to understand that the down-stroke is aimed forward. And because the motivating balance is in the back, it is the upper-arm (the outer, heavier side) that follows up the motivating force and transmits the stroke. The movement of the elbow, fore-arm, wrist and fingers are only a natural follow-up to the lead of the upper arm. At the end of the down-stroke the arm should be straight forward from the shoulder (there are always a few exceptions, depending on arm length). This forward motion is necessary because the bow will become gradually lighter towards the tip and the increasing weight of the 'forward' moving arm (transmitted through the hand onto the stick) will supplement the decreasing weight of the bow and will take care of an even tone production. And because of this *natural* weight of the whole arm, there will be no need to apply artificial pressure from the index finger and hand. Also the bow can remain parallel with the bridge throughout the stroke.

THE UP-STROKE

Now just as the bow becomes increasingly lighter towards the tip on the down-stroke—so it becomes increasingly heavier towards the nut on the up-stroke. This causes one of the most serious problems for beginners, (and for many good players as well). For the increasing weight of the bow on the up-stroke, as well as that of the hand and arm, create an ugly sound towards the end of the stroke. And this is the reason for most of the screeching—and anxiety —which beginners think they have to endure. In self defence, either they avoid using this part of the bow altogether, or when they get there, they try to lighten the pressure by lifting the bow from the 'hand'. Understandable as this intention is, it immediately stiffens the fingers and the bow-stroke becomes a trembling uncertainty.

So, just as with the down-stroke, it should be the *whole* arm and *not* the fore-arm and hand which make the necessary adjustments. This time the weight of the fore-arm must *decrease* to such an extent that by the end of the stroke it can return to the 'floating' sensation so that there is no weight (and certainly no pressure whatsoever) on the bow from the fore-arm and hand. But remember that there is an enormous difference between 'lifting' the arm and 'floating' it. (see page 10).

In order to *decrease* the weight of the fore-arm and hand on the up-stroke, the imaginary weight in the back and factual weight of the outer side of the upper-arm should *increase* in proportion as a counter-balance. And just as the arm in the down-stroke opens forward, so the up-stroke completely reverses the movement without any effort from the fore-arm. It is the upper-arm and the elbow that 'scoop' inward against the body and help to raise the fore-arm and hand. If the wrist is as loose as it should be (see page 7) it will flex with the bow-stroke and end up on the same level as the hand, or perhaps even higher. Please make certain that the wrist and the arm are turned towards the violin all the time. For this is the only way in which the tip of the little finger can rest on the bow. This is vital, for the balance of the little finger plays an important role in the bow-hold whilst playing at the nut. (see bow-hold (p. 6, 7).

All these details may sound complicated at first, but in fact they are not. For if the mind is trained from the very beginning to focus only on the key points of balance the remaining movements will come automatically. So let us simplify the intricate balances of the bow-stroke again by going back to the idea of the see-saw. Your body is the pivot. The imaginary weight in the shoulder-blade is the heavy end, and the arm representing the light end opens and shuts as though on a spring.

EXERCISE 7

Repeat the following exercises twelve times without, and twelve times with the bow alone. (No violin).
1. DROP YOUR RIGHT ARM BESIDE YOUR BODY AND FIND THE BOW-HOLD.
2. BEND YOUR RIGHT ARM AT THE ELBOW AND SUSPEND IT (PALM DOWNWARDS) FROM THE WEIGHT IN THE BACK, TO FIND THE 'FLOATING' SENSATION IN THE FORE-ARM AND HAND.
3. TURN YOUR FORE-ARM AND WRIST TOWARDS THE LEFT.
4. LET THE DOWN-STROKE OPEN FROM THE *UPPER-ARM* DOWN

THROUGH THE ELBOW FORE-ARM AND WRIST IN A FORWARD
MOTION UNTIL THE ARM IS COMPLETELY STRETCHED.

5. 'SCOOP' THE *UPPER-ARM* INWARDS TO RETURN WITH THE UP-
STROKE, DROPPING THE ELBOW AND FLEXING THE WRIST UNTIL
YOUR FORE-ARM HAS RETURNED TO THE ORIGINAL 'FLOATING'
POSITION.

Make certain that the movement of the fore-arm, wrist and hand is only a
follow-up of the upper-arm and not a lead.

EXERCISE 8

BEFORE THE BOW-STROKE IS TRIED ON THE VIOLIN ITSELF,
MAKE CERTAIN THAT THE VIOLIN-HOLD IS RIGHT. GO THROUGH
THE MOVEMENTS STEP BY STEP FOR HOLDING THE VIOLIN. (pp. 4, 5,
6). IF NECESSARY REPEAT THESE EXERCISES SEVERAL TIMES BE-
FORE GOING ON. IT IS VERY GOOD TRAINING NEVER TO RUSH INTO
PLAYING, BUT TO MAKE SURE EACH TIME YOU BEGIN, THAT EVERY
SINGLE BALANCE IS RIGHT. AND ONLY WHEN THE VIOLIN-HOLD
SEEMS QUITE COMFORTABLE TRY THE BOW-HOLD.

FIRST TRY THE BOW-HOLD WITH THE STICK IN A VERTICAL
POSITION. MAKE QUITE CERTAIN THAT THE MUSCLE UNDER THE
THUMB IS COMPLETELY LOOSE. THEN LIFT YOUR UPPER-ARM
ALMOST TO THE LEVEL OF YOUR SHOULDER WITH THE FORE-ARM
TURNED TOWARDS THE VIOLIN, (BUT DO NOT RAISE THE SHOULDER
ITSELF) AND POISE THE BOW AT THE NUT ABOVE THE G STRING.

In order to avoid the fear of the horrible crunchy sound which the heaviness
of the bow and hand causes here, make certain that the imaginary weight in the
back assures a floating sensation in the front.

Repeat this 'getting readiness', this co-ordination of violin-hold and bow-
hold, until the anxiety is eliminated and the violin and bow seem like natural
extensions of the body because of your reliance on the fundamental balances.

EXERCISE 9

ONCE THIS 'GETTING READINESS' IS WELL ESTABLISHED, WITH
THE BOW POISED OVER THE G STRING, MAKE CERTAIN THAT THE
MOMENTUM OF THE STROKE WILL IN FACT BEGIN IN THE UPPER
ARM WHICH IS ALMOST LEVEL WITH THE SHOULDER AND *NOT* IN
THE HAND. A GOOD EXERCISE FOR THIS (STILL WITHOUT THE BOW
ACTUALLY TOUCHING THE STRING) IS TO SWING THE UPPER-ARM
DOWNWARDS TOWARDS YOUR BODY (WITH THE FORE-ARM AND
HAND STILL TURNED TOWARDS THE VIOLIN) AND THEN SWING
IT OUT AND UP ABOVE THE G STRING AGAIN. YOU WILL SEE THAT
A SWIFT REPETITION OF THIS MOVEMENT IN THE UPPER-ARM WILL
CREATE A CIRCLE AND WILL ESTABLISH THE FREEDOM OF THE
STROKE. IF THIS MOVEMENT SEEMS DIFFICULT, TRY IT WITHOUT
THE BOW FIRST. THINK ABOUT IT—AND THEN TRY IT WITH THE
BOW AGAIN. IT SHOULD BE A BIG SWINGING MOVEMENT WITH NO
RESTRAINT.

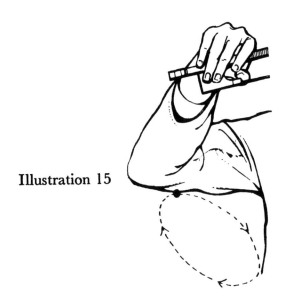

Illustration 15

THE THUMB

Though the momentum of the bow-stroke is in the upper arm—the completion of the movement is in the thumb, in the tip of the bent 2nd joint. It is most important that the movement should not finish in the fingers. For if the fingers take on the movement, they are bound to create pressure on the stick. And a good tone is never produced by force. Good tone is the result of friction which is caused by the resin on the bow-hair which set the string vibrating.
(see A NEW APPROACH TO VIOLIN PLAYING, pp.25-26.)

So the completion of the bow-stroke is in the *bent* 2nd joint of the thumb which is underneath the stick and can not create pressure on the string. Therefore it is not only in a strategic position for guiding the bow, but it can also control the volume of tone without the danger of creating harshness. Indeed this bent joint is like the tip of a paintbrush on canvas in its ability to shade and colour the tone with great delicacy.

EXERCISE 10

1. CO-ORDINATE THE VIOLIN-HOLD AND BOW-HOLD (WITH THE STICK IN VERTICAL POSITION) RELYING ON THE SEE-SAW IMAGE.
2. TILT THE BOW OVER THE VIOLIN. TRY OUT THE CIRCULAR EXERCISE WITH THE UPPER-ARM TO ASSURE FREEDOM.
3. LIFT THE UPPER-ARM ALMOST TO THE LEVEL OF THE SHOULDER; FEEL THE IMAGINARY WEIGHT IN THE SHOULDER-BLADE EXTENDING TO IT, TO ESTABLISH THE 'FLOATING' POSITION OF FORE-ARM AND HAND ABOVE THE 'G' STRING.
4. BEGIN THE MOVEMENT OF THE STROKE IN MID-AIR A LITTLE BEYOND WHERE THE HAIR JOINS THE NUT. THE MOVEMENT IS FROM THE UPPER-ARM. DROP THE BOW LIGHTLY (JUST WHERE THE HAIR BEGINS) ON THE STRING, THEN, RELYING ON THE FEELING OF WEIGHT IN THE BACK, GUIDE THE STROKE WITH THE *BENT* JOINT OF THE THUMB UNDERNEATH THE STICK. *THE BOW MUST BE PARALLEL WITH THE BRIDGE THROUGHOUT THE STROKE.*

THE STROKE BEGINS STRAIGHT, BUT THEN FROM THE MIDDLE OF THE BOW, SLOWLY GUIDE IT FORWARD AWAY FROM THE BODY, WITH THE FEELING THAT THE THUMB (BENT OUTWARD) IS *PULLING* THE WEIGHT OF THE BOW. REVERSE THIS MOVEMENT FOR THE UP-STROKE, SO THAT THIS TIME THE THUMB *PUSHES* THE WEIGHT OF THE BOW. TRY THIS SIX TIMES WITHOUT ANY MUSIC AT FIRST. THEN KEEP YOUR EYES ON THE MUSIC AND COUNT FOUR *VERY* SLOW BEATS FOR EACH NOTE.

CHANGE OF BOW

The thumb is loose and pliable throughout the strokes. The extent to which it should bend cannot be rigidly decreed, for it depends on the shape and size of the thumb which varies with each individual. In some cases it may have to straighten a little at the end of the down-stroke. When this happens, extra care should be taken that it bends again during the up-stroke. This jutting outward position of the thumb is of the greatest importance because it is not only the perfect antidote to 'clutching' the bow, but a smooth bow change entirely depends on it too. For the momentum in the arm will end each stroke in the *curve* of the thumb. This produces a tiny upward curve of the bow at the end of every down-stroke giving the note a chance to be completely finished before the up-stroke is taken on the return of the same curve.

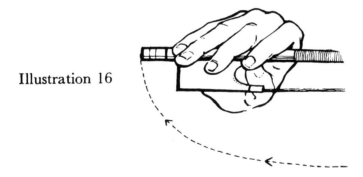

Illustration 16

Exactly the same thing happens at the end of the up-stroke. The momentum of the 'scooping' and folding back of the arm also finishes in the curve of the thumb at the nut before the down-stroke takes over.

Illustration 17

In order to achieve a completely smooth bow-change, it is most important to realize that the strokes are like the "lower half of a large circle."

15

EXERCISE 11

CHECK ALL THE POINTS IN THE PREVIOUS EXERCISE CAREFULLY AND PLAY THE FOLLOWING WITH EXAGGERATED SLOWNESS SO THAT YOU KNOW *EXACTLY* WHAT YOU ARE DOING. *LEARN TO LISTEN ALL THE TIME.* FOR THE SOUND WILL TELL YOU WHETHER YOU ARE DOING WELL OR NOT. IF THE SOUND IS HARSH OR UNPLEASANT, STOP. CHECK ALL THE BALANCES ONCE MORE, STEP BY STEP, ONLY THEN BEGIN AGAIN. FOR IF ALL THE BALANCES ARE CORRECT AND NO ARTIFICIAL FORCE IS USED, THE VIOLIN SHOULD PRODUCE A LOVELY SOUND RIGHT FROM THE VERY BEGINNING. THE IMPORTANT THING IS NEVER TO BE IMPATIENT BUT TO LEARN TO *THINK* AND *LISTEN*, AND TO REMEMBER THAT NO PART OF THE BODY CAN DO ANYTHING WITHOUT AN ORDER FROM THE MIND.

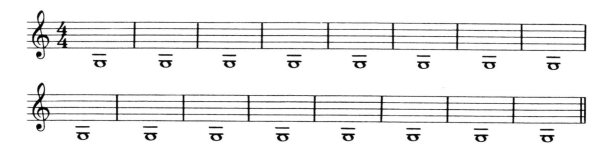

EXERCISE 12

PUT THE VIOLIN DOWN, HANG YOUR ARMS LOOSELY BY YOUR SIDE AND REST A SECOND. THEN REPEAT EXERCISE 9 BUT NOW POISE THE UPPER-ARM AND BOW ABOVE THE D STRING. THE UPPER-ARM IS IN A LOWER POSITION NOW, FOR THE D STRING IS ON A DIFFERENT LEVEL FROM THE G STRING.

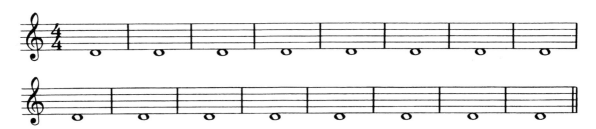

Put down the violin. Hang your arms and rest a second.

EXERCISE 13

REPEAT EXERCISE 10. POISE THE UPPER ARM AND BOW ABOVE THE LEVEL OF THE A STRING WHICH IS IN A *MUCH* LOWER POSITION THAN THE D STRING. MANY BEGINNERS FIND THE A STRING DIFFICULT BECAUSE THEY DO NOT MAKE THE NECESSARY LEVELLING ADJUSTMENT IN THE UPPER ARM, ESPECIALLY IF THEY DO NOT SCOOP DEEPLY ENOUGH IN THE UP-STROKE. (see p.12).

16

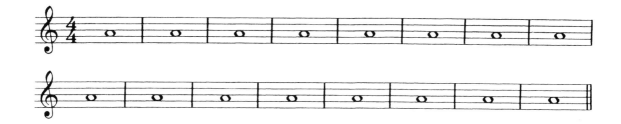

EXERCISE 14

PUT DOWN THE VIOLIN AGAIN. HANG YOUR ARMS AND REST. THEN REPEAT EXERCISE 10, BUT THIS TIME THE UPPER ARM AND BOW IS POISED TO THE CORRECT LEVEL OF THE E STRING WHICH IS VERY LOW INDEED, SO THE UPPER-ARM IS ALMOST NEXT TO THE BODY. DO EXAGGERATE THE 'SCOOPING' MOVEMENT IN THE UP-STROKE OTHERWISE YOU WILL NOT FIND THE BALANCE, AND THE STROKE WILL BE UNSTEADY. (See p.12 again.)

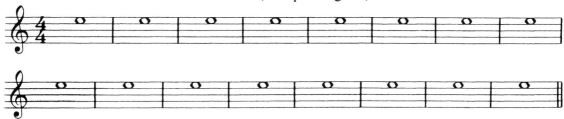

ADVICE FOR PRACTISING

I cannot emphasize enough how important it is to do the right sort of work between lessons. Even though you understand each point, the co-ordination of them all would still create anxiety because everything is very new and it is a lot to assimilate. And this anxiety would be transmitted to your playing.

On the other hand the results will be amazingly good if you do some *silent* work every day. Go over all the exercises from 1 to 11 with great care without the violin and bow. Never force anything. Do realize that you are trying to train your mind, not your body. Once the mind learns to give the right orders to the right places, your body will have no alternative but to obey. So to assure rapid progress and good playing, what you must learn at the moment is *how* to work in your mind.

NOTE TO THE ADVANCED PLAYER

As you will see later, once you understand the principle of the 'floating' arm and the 'scoop' with the importance of the 'paint-brush' thumb you have conquered the principle of all bowing technique, including the détaché, spiccato, martelè, etc.

I would like to emphasise again that nothing can gauge the correctness of the balance better than the slow open string bowing. If the stroke has even the slightest tremble, it is a certain sign of faulty application. But if the balances are well established you can count 30 slowly for one stroke and will feel that the length of the bow is still endless.

The correct playing of slow, open string bowing at the beginning of each practice is one of the greatest helps towards achieving control and eliminating anxiety and it is an invaluable "nerve-steadier" before a performance.

L E S S O N III

STRING CROSSING

Before continuing, let us summarise the major points and repeat the exercises on which good violin playing depends.

1. THE SOURCE OF THE FUNDAMENTAL BALANCES WHICH ELIMINATE ANXIETY. (p.1).

   The see-saw image. (p.3).

   The 'suspended' 'floating' arms. (p. 3-12).

2. *MENTAL DISCIPLINE*. (p.2).

   The control and co-ordination of the fundamental balances. (p.2).

3. REPEAT EXERCISES 1 and 2 (p. 4) SIX TIMES WITHOUT THE VIOLIN AND SIX TIMES WITH IT.

4. TRY OUT THE VIOLIN-HOLD, REPEAT EXERCISE 3 (p. 5). SIX TIMES WITHOUT THE VIOLIN AND SIX TIMES WITH IT.

5. TRY OUT THE BOW-HOLD WITHOUT THE BOW (p. 6). REPEAT EXERCISE 4 (p. 8) SIX TIMES THEN REPEAT EXERCISE 5 (p. 8) SIX TIMES.

6. REPEAT EXERCISE 7 (p.12) TWELVE TIMES WITHOUT THE BOW AND TWELVE TIMES WITH IT.

7. NOW GET READY TO PLAY ACCORDING TO EXERCISE 9, THEN REPEAT EXERCISE 10.

The strokes should be *very* slow indeed because that is the only way to establish real control.

EXERCISE 15

Stop and rest. Think about and then practise the seven points as before, to establish the 'floating' position of the fore-arm and hand, and only then go on, this time on the D string. Be careful to lower the level of your upper-arm for the D string.

Stop and rest. Think about, and then practise, the seven points on the A string. Make certain to lower the level of your upper-arm for the A string.

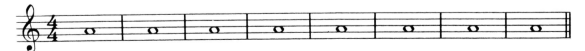

Rest. Think about, and practise, the seven points on the E string. Lower your upper arm until it is almost next to your body for the E string.

Rest. Go over *EXERCISE* 9 (p.13) and then continue.

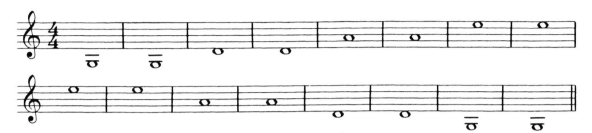

Whenever you do not feel absolutely at ease, check on the violin-hold, then check on the bow-hold. *Make certain that the right thumb is bent outward and that the fore-arm and the hand are turned toward the violin.*

If the strokes seem even the slightest bit uncertain, check on the 'floating' position in the down-stroke and the 'scooping' movement in the up-stroke. Remember to change the position of your upper-arm when crossing from string to string. Remember to guide the bow forward with the thumb on the down-stroke.

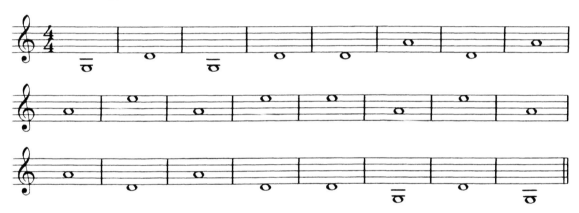

Rest a second. *Think* about the seven points. Remember that if you do not feel at ease or if the sound is not clear and full (*feeling at ease and good sound always go together*) a slight adjustment of the feeling of weight in the back or in the upper-arm may make all the difference. *Do not clutch the bow with your fingers.*

In the following exercises make certain that the string crossing is always from the upper-arm, never from the fore-arm.

Do not forget to 'scoop' when you raise the upper-arm for the lower sounding strings.

The following exercises are in minims. As there are only two beats for each stroke, the strokes have to be swifter. *It is very important to realize that the swift*

strokes are prepared with exactly the same care and depend on exactly the same balances as the slow strokes.

The difference between the slow and swift stroke is in the energy of the momentum which sets the stroke in motion, i.e. the upper-arm. On no account must the fore-arm take over control. (See p. 11, 12).

Get ready to play according to EXERCISE 9.

Remember to lower your *upper-arm* for the D string.

Remember to lower your *upper-arm* for the A string.

Remember to hang down your upper-arm for the E string.

If the stroke seems uneasy or stiff, or if the sound is rough—watch out for the following points.

1. Check on your bow-hold.
2. Make certain your fore-arm and hand are turned toward the violin.
3. Make sure that your right thumb is bent *outward* enough.
4. Check on the 'scoop'. Is there enough on the up-stroke?

Remember string crossing is from the *upper-arm.*

Repeat the same exercises in crotchets. As there is only one beat for each stroke, the strokes are now quite swift.

Please remember again that the swift strokes are prepared with exactly the same care and depend on exactly the same balances as the slow strokes. But now, instead of making a gradual opening movement, 'throw forward' your upper-arm in the down-stroke and drop it backwards in a sudden 'scoop' in the up-stroke. If the bow-hold is correct and if the wrist is loose, the swift strokes become an effortless 'swinging' motion, self propelled. (See Change of Bow p.15).

Get ready to play according to EXERCISE 9 (p.13).

Remember to lower your *upper-arm* for the D string.

Remember to lower your *upper-arm* for the A string.

Remember to hang down your *upper-arm* for the E string.

Remember to : —
1. Check on your bow-hold.
2. Make certain your fore-arm and hand are turned towards the violin.
3. Make certain your right thumb is bent outward enough.
4. Check whether the 'scoop' is enough on the up-stroke.

Remember string crossing is from the *upper-arm*.

NOTE TO ADVANCED PLAYERS

The playing of the swift open string bowing should be another daily exercise following immediately after the slow open string bowing. The 'thrown-forward' down-stroke and the sudden 'scoop' on the up-stroke is a most wonderful liberating exercise after the severe control of the slow bowing.

Please follow these exercises with the left hand action in Lesson V.

LESSON IV

CONSOLIDATION OF THE OPEN STRING BOWING

Please do not rush into playing, but get used to preparing each action before beginning. If you learn to establish the fundamental balances at the start, the advancement will be rapid, for all technique depends on these. Please remember that violin playing should never develop into an endurance test: but that it is a pleasurable means of creating music. This begins right at the start with the open strings. Do not say to yourself "Never mind what these sound like; these are only open strings," because to create a beautiful sound is equally important at any stage of violin playing. And the degree of pleasure you create for the listener depends a great deal on how much pleasure you get out of it yourself. Speaking for myself, I would much rather hear a beginner really enjoying himself on the open strings, making full use of all the musical possibilities, than hear somebody hacking away at the Beethoven Concerto making use of nothing.

Summarize the major points again before beginning to play.

1. THE SOURCE OF THE FUNDAMENTAL BALANCES WHICH ELIM- INATE ANXIETY.
   The see-saw image (p.3).
   The 'suspended' 'floating' arm (**p. 3 & p. 12**).

2. MENTAL DISCIPLINE (p.2).

3. REPEAT EXERCISES 1 AND 2 SIX TIMES WITHOUT THE VIOLIN AND SIX TIMES WITH IT.

4. TRY OUT THE VIOLIN-HOLD, REPEAT EXERCISE 3 SIX TIMES WITHOUT THE VIOLIN AND SIX TIMES WITH IT.

5. TRY OUT THE BOW-HOLD WITHOUT THE BOW (p. 6). REPEAT EXERCISE 4 SIX TIMES, THEN EXERCISE 5 SIX TIMES.

6. REPEAT EXERCISE 7 TWELVE TIMES WITHOUT THE BOW AND TWELVE TIMES WITH IT.

7. NOW GET READY TO PLAY ACCORDING TO EXERCISE 10. STOP AND REST

EXERCISE 16

Sing each of the following exercises and instead of singing 'la' sing the notes counting out the beats. Then play each exercise alone first, and only then with the accompaniment.

EXERCISE 17

24

EXERCISE 18

EXERCISE 19

USE THE WHOLE LENGTH OF THE BOW WITH EACH STROKE AND MAKE CERTAIN THAT THE UPPER-ARM IS FREE TO LIFT AND DROP ACCORDING TO THE DEMANDS OF THE STRING CROSSING. REMEMBER THAT THE RESTS ARE AS IMPORTANT AS THE NOTES.

EXERCISE 20

The lowering and lifting of the upper-arm must be very swift when crossing from the G to the E string and back from the E string to the G string etc. in order to avoid the sounds of the strings in between.

EXERCISE 21

PUT AWAY THE VIOLIN AND PLEASE DO NOT TOUCH IT UNTIL THE NEXT LESSON.

LESSON V

THE LEFT HAND

The importance of the fundamental balances, when it comes to the left hand action, is incalculable. For, while the control of length of sound, its smoothness and its volume, is in the bowing arm, the *quality* of tone depends entirely on the left hand action—that is, to use a pianistic term—on the touch (SEE A NEW APPROACH TO VIOLIN PLAYING (p.28)). And a perfect touch is impossible without making full use of the fundamental balances. So, before going any further, check on the stance and on the violin-hold again and make certain that there is no tension in the left arm (see p.4 & 5).

Now try the following without the violin.

Drop your left arm next to your body and note what a considerable distance there is between the thumb and the index finger. There is even a web-like skin between them which nature has provided. There is a much greater distance between them than between any of the other fingers and the motion of the tip of the index finger falling somewhere on the inside of the thumb nearer the hand creates the opening and closing of a circle. The exact size of this circle—that is—the exact point of contact between the tip of the index finger and the side of the thumb, depends on the shape of the player's hand; but generally speaking the tip of the index finger is somewhere below the 2nd joint of the thumb.

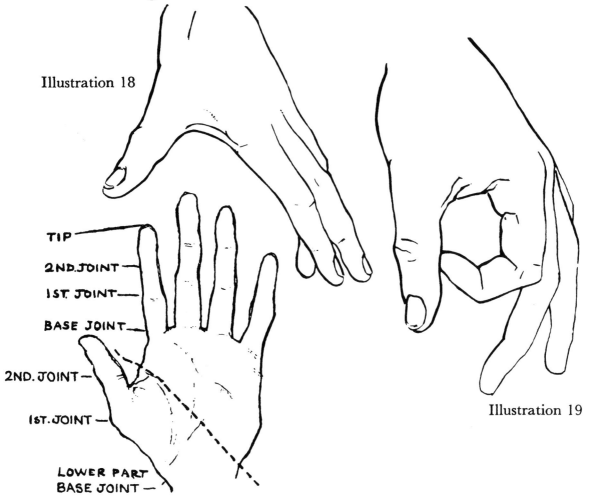

Illustration 18

TIP
2ND. JOINT
1ST JOINT
BASE JOINT
2ND. JOINT
1ST. JOINT
LOWER PART
BASE JOINT

Illustration 19

The creation of this circle between the thumb and index finger is one of the most important points in violin playing because it assures the freedom of movement of the fingers above the fingerboard; for it prevents the thumb and the side of the index finger from clamping together under the neck, one of the most common pitfalls of a beginner. The thumb is light and flexible while the 2nd joint is in continuous contact with the neck. Because if it is not, there is a danger of the thumb becoming a prop for the violin. Apart from that, the exact position of the thumb varies with each player depending on the size of his hand.

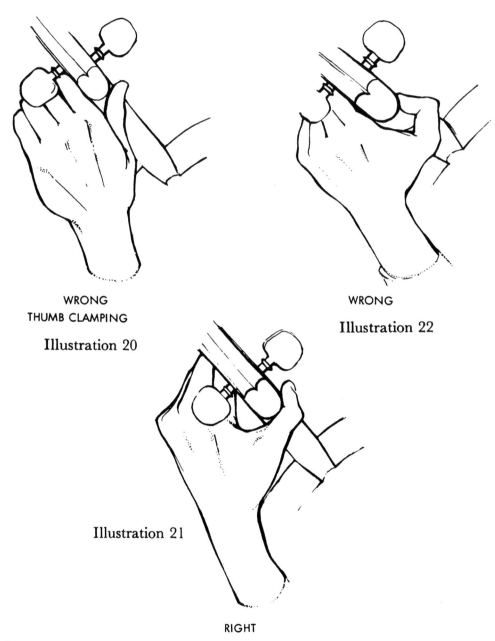

WRONG
THUMB CLAMPING

Illustration 20

WRONG

Illustration 22

Illustration 21

RIGHT

Keep this circle between the thumb and the index finger, then 'suspend' your left arm with the palm facing you as if playing the violin (see p.4). Lift the index finger as high as possible until it is straight, then drop it lightly, by a *forward* action, onto the thumb. The wrist is straight between the hand and the (DRAWING 23) arm and *completely loose*. Do not bend it backwards (DRAWING 24) or forward (DRAWING 25) and do not twist it towards the thumb (DRAWING 26). It should be opposite your face while the rest of the fingers are lightly bent at all joints, *including the base joints*.

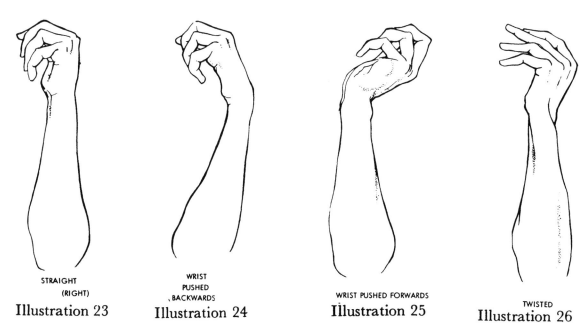

STRAIGHT
(RIGHT)

Illustration 23

WRIST
PUSHED
BACKWARDS

Illustration 24

WRIST PUSHED FORWARDS

Illustration 25

TWISTED

Illustration 26

If the wrist is completely loose and straight and if the natural distance between thumb and index finger is utilized, you will see that the fingers are slightly bent by nature in every joint, including the base joints. The index or first finger is the highest, while the others curl lower and lower as if they were a descending staircase (DRAWING 27). This relaxed free position will be invaluable later on in the changing of position, glissando, double stops, etc.

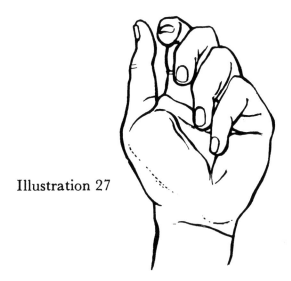

Illustration 27

Make certain that the action of the index finger onto the side of the thumb is always a *forward motion* towards you and that the left elbow points to the ground and is not twisted under the violin. This forward motion of the index finger is a most important point and deserves special attention. For the tendency of most players is to twist the hand towards the neck of the violin when trying to raise the fingers above the strings, simply because the finger-board is to be left of the hand.

Lift the index finger again and throw it first towards the left with a twisted hand and then forward with the hand straight, and see what a difference there is between the two actions. There is many an advanced player whose difficulties are solved immediately following the correction of this tendency of twisting the hand to the left, when faced with tricky passages.

EXERCISE 22

DROP YOUR LEFT ARM NEXT TO YOUR BODY WITH THE PALM FACING YOUR SIDE. STRAIGHTEN THE INDEX FINGER: THEN DROP IT ONTO THE INSIDE OF THE THUMB. TRY THIS TWELVE TIMES. 'SUSPEND' YOUR LEFT ARM AS IF HOLDING THE VIOLIN. TRY THE SAME EXERCISE TWELVE TIMES IN THAT POSITION.

As for the actual tone production—or 'touch' itself; it cannot be repeated enough that the core of all violin playing is in a beautiful tone; because only through that, through a quality of tone, which has the power to move, can one find a true artistic outlet.

As we have seen before, the principle idea of the fundamental balances is that of concentrating on the 'source' of each movement, the place where the motivating force originates. For this motivating force, by its fundamental power, controls all the lesser movements involved as well; so that every movement, down to the smallest one, is the natural result of a basic power and no superimposed force is ever necessary.

The motivating power, as we have seen with the right arm motion, is not always visible. This fact is especially true when it comes to the left finger action. To the eye the left finger-tip seems so authoritative when in contact with the string, that many violinists' attention tends to be focused on the finger-tip itself. But as our fingers are some of the smallest and weakest parts of our whole body, it stands to reason that it would be a mistake to overburden them with the responsibility of all the technical problems which violin playing entails, such as rapid passages, big stretches, etc. So, because of the paramount importance of the correct understanding of this, let us underline again the difference between causes and effects. Without the cause, i.e. the motivating power, it would not be possible for the effect, i.e. the movement itself, to take place. So, however authoritative the effect seems by itself, (i.e. the left finger action) the natural power, the real control, lies in the cause. And in the case of the left finger action the motivating power is way back in the *base joints*.

The actual source of the finger-action is around the elbow joint (DRAWING 28) but the nearest balance point of leverage which has the power to control is in the base joints.

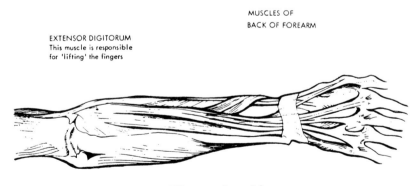

MUSCLES OF
BACK OF FOREARM

EXTENSOR DIGITORUM
This muscle is responsible
for 'lifting' the fingers

Illustration 28

Stretch your hand, then bend only the first and second joints of the index finger and feel the muscle running up that side of the hand. It is stiff. No circle is possible, and the whole hand is tense.

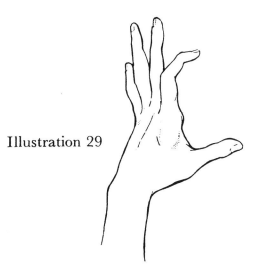

Illustration 29

Now bend the index finger from the base joint and see how relaxed the muscle is how the other fingers will want to bend too, and how the circle is formed quite naturally.

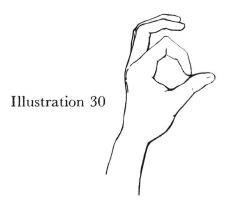

Illustration 30

From the point of view of tone production, one must know that each note is a compound sound consisting of the ground note and of its harmonics. Now if the note is played as a direct 'hit' on the string from the finger-tip, the full play of the compound sound wave systems is disturbed and a hard dead sound is the result. Also, if there is a direct vertical pressure on the string in order to retain the stop, the thumb must also press up or against the neck to support this strain, and a stiff thumb gripping the neck is one of the greatest handicaps to good violin playing. But if the finger-action is merely the effect of a throw from the base joint, the contact of the finger-tip on the string is light and sensitive, because the very distance between the base joint and the string makes an immediate pressure on the finger-board impossible. Consequently, while the thumb remains a mobile point of balance, the two most important elements of tone production (apart from the freeplay of overtones) become combined—a faultless intonation and a spontaneous vibrato.

I said in the beginning that the aim of this approach is to eliminate anxiety. And one of the most deeply rooted anxieties in violin playing is caused by intonation. There is the whole length of the finger-board (thinks the beginner) and just where exactly *is* that 'A' with the first finger on the G string? There are no frets on the violin, no indication of any kind as to where the notes should go; and knowing the approximate distance of the 'A' from the nut does

31

not assure correct intonation, because violin playing is so sensitive that even a fraction of an inch makes all the difference between being in tune and being out of tune. Anyway a tape-measured mentality is not the best road to artistic expression.

However, as we shall see, with the resilience and lightness of the touch (because it is controlled from the base joint) the finger is flexible, the finger-tip sensitive, and there is a spontaneous adjustment the moment the finger is in contact with the string. So, instead of the continuous worry of being in tune, intonation becomes part of tone production.

At the same time, the energy generating from the base joint also assures a vibrato which does not depend on the oscillation of the hand and arm. For this energy in the base joint, which is transmitted via the finger onto the string, is a *natural* weight on the string and the play-action of its fundamental balance creates a vibrato which is as spontaneous and phenomenal as only creative art can be. And it is wonderful to hear how all the beauty in the instrument immediately responds to it.

Once this point is well understood, violin playing becomes a continuous pleasure and reward even at the very beginning. It is important to realize that the difficulty in violin playing is not physical. The difficulty lies in the mental acceptance of taking away responsibility from the seemingly obvious (i.e. the fingers) and in the mental discipline of handing it on to the seemingly obscure. (i.e. the base joints.)

In order to develop this energy in the base joint you must be able to forget about the fingers completely; so when teaching, I hardly ever refer to the fingers, but only to the base joints.

EXERCISE 23
DROP YOUR ARM NEXT TO YOUR BODY WITH THE PALM FACING YOUR SIDE. THEN SLOWLY CURL YOUR FINGERS INTO YOUR PALM. DO THIS VERY SLOWLY AND WHILE THE FINGERS ARE CURLING, FOCUS YOUR ATTENTION ON THE BASE JOINTS AND IMAGINE FOUR SOUNDS OOZING OUT OF THEIR CURVATURES AS THE RESULT OF THIS MOVEMENT, THE SAME SORT OF LAZY SOUND WHICH AN ACCORDIAN WOULD PRODUCE WHEN IN SLOW MOTION. REPEAT TWELVE TIMES.

EXERCISE 24
FIND AN 'A' ABOVE MIDDLE C ON THE PIANO, OR WITH A TUNING FORK—LISTEN TO IT CAREFULLY FIRST, THEN SING OR HUM IT. DO NOT SAY 'LA' OR 'MM' BUT SAY 'A' WHILE YOU SING IT.

EXERCISE 25
DROP YOUR LEFT ARM NEXT TO YOUR BODY WITH THE PALM FACING YOUR SIDE. CREATE A CIRCLE BETWEEN THE INDEX FIN-

GER AND THE THUMB. STRAIGHTEN THE INDEX FINGER FROM THE BASE JOINT AND SING 'A' AGAIN, AND IMAGINE THAT THE *SOUND*, THE *NAME* AND THE *FEELING* OF THAT 'A' ARE ONE AND THE SAME THING INHABITING THE BONE OF THE LIFTED BASE JOINT. TRY TO IMAGINE THIS SO STRONGLY THAT EVEN WHEN YOU DROP YOUR FINGER FROM THE BASE JOINT ONTO THE THUMB AGAIN, IT FEELS AS IF IT WERE HELD BACK BY THE WEIGHT OF THIS LIVING 'A'. DO THIS EXERCISE TWELVE TIMES AND TRY TO PLACE THE WEIGHT OF THE 'A' MORE AND MORE INTO THE BASE JOINT.

EXERCISE 26

DROP YOUR ARM NEXT TO YOUR BODY WITH THE PALM FACING YOUR SIDE. CREATE A CIRCLE BETWEEN THE INDEX FINGER AND THE THUMB. LIFT THE INDEX FINGER FROM THE BASE JOINT, BUT THIS TIME, INSTEAD OF SINGING THE 'A' ALOUD, TRY TO *HEAR* IT! HEAR THE SOUND WITH THE NAME; THAT IS, MAKE CERTAIN THAT YOU ARE NOT HEARING JUST ANY SOUND, BUT THAT YOU ARE HEARING A DISTINCT 'A' SOUND, WHICH IS LITERALLY SWELLING WITH LIFE IN YOUR BASE JOINT. THEN DROP THE FINGER FORWARD AGAIN FROM THE BASE JOINT. REPEAT THIS EXERCISE TWELVE TIMES. BUT PLEASE STOP AS SOON AS YOU DO NOT HEAR THE 'A'. SOUND IT AND SING IT AGAIN, AND ONLY THEN CONTINUE. REST FREQUENTLY; DO NOT TRY TO RUSH IT TOO HARD BECAUSE THIS EXERCISE DEMANDS GREAT CONCENTRATION AND CAN BE VERY TIRING.

EXERCISE 27

SUSPEND YOUR LEFT ARM AS IF HOLDING THE VIOLIN. MAKE CERTAIN THAT THE ELBOW POINTS TO THE GROUND AND THAT YOUR WRIST IS STRAIGHT AND COMPLETELY LOOSE FACING TOWARDS YOU. OPEN THE DISTANCE BETWEEN THUMB AND INDEX FINGER. LET YOUR FINGERS CURL NATURALLY IN THE SHAPE OF THE DESCENDING STAIRCASE. LIFT THE INDEX FINGER FROM THE BASE JOINT, *HEAR* AN 'A' (IF YOU CANNOT HEAR IT FIND IT AGAIN ON THE PIANO OR WITH A TUNING FORK, SING IT AN OCTAVE LOWER AND THEN TRY TO HEAR IT) AND PLACE THE *NAME*, THE *SOUND* AND THE *FEELING* OF THAT 'A' INTO THE BONE OF THE LIFTED BASE JOINT. THEN AS BEFORE, DROP THE FINGER FORWARD FROM IT ONTO THE THUMB RETAINING THE ENERGY IN THE BASE JOINT: OR IT MAY HELP TO CONJURE UP A DIFFERENT PICTURE. TRY TO IMAGINE THAT 'A' SO STRONGLY AGAIN THAT THOUGH THE MOVEMENT IS FORWARD, THE BONE OF THE BASE JOINT ITSELF FEELS AS IF IT WERE KEPT TILTED BACK BECAUSE OF THE WEIGHT OF THAT 'A'. REPEAT IT TWELVE TIMES. BUT MAKE CERTAIN THAT THE WRIST AND THE ARM DO NOT STIFFEN OR TWIST DURING THIS EXERCISE.

These exercises are most important because they are really a training of the mind (which of course includes the ear). For, they are either impossible to do, or become silly nonsense, unless full concentration is applied. It can not be repeated enough that violin playing is a form of creative art and not a mechanical process. And just as the story of an author, or the painting of an artist is conceived in the mind long before paper or canvas is touched, so for a violinist the sound should be a living conception long before the fingers even feel the string. This pre-conception is not a question of talent—it is merely a matter of training. It may seem difficult in the beginning, but with systematic and patient training it will develop surprisingly well. And the fusion of the two, both of feeling and of hearing the sound *before* touching it, eliminates the long stages of mechanical struggle with the fingers, to which so many violinists are exposed.

In order to make the sound 'come out of you', so to speak, it is important to concentrate on only one note at a time in the beginning—such as that 'A'. If you have difficulties with the 'feeling' of it in the base joint, rub the base joint gently with the right hand while you sing the 'A'. For many people this physical contact is a great help in pin-pointing the mind.

EXERCISE 28

HOLD THE VIOLIN, THEN TOSS IT ON YOUR COLLAR-BONE. MAKE CERTAIN THAT THE VIOLIN HOLD IS LIGHT, BALANCED AND COMPLETELY SECURE. THIS IS MOST IMPORTANT BECAUSE THIS IS THE ONLY WAY TO ENSURE THAT THE LEFT ARM AND THE THUMB WILL NOT FEEL THE NEED TO SUPPORT THE VIOLIN.

DROP YOUR LEFT ARM NEXT TO YOUR BODY, THEN SWING IT BACK AND FORTH BY YOUR SIDE AS IF WALKING TO ENSURE ITS FREEDOM. PLEASE DO NOT GO ON UNTIL THIS EXERCISE FEELS EASY.

FORM A CIRCLE BETWEEN THUMB AND INDEX FINGER. 'SUSPEND' THE ARM UNDER THE VIOLIN, ENCIRCLING THE NECK WITH THE THUMB AND INDEX FINGER. MAKE CERTAIN THAT THE WRIST IS STRAIGHT AND LOOSE, (see p.29) AND MAKE CERTAIN THAT THE 2ND JOINT OF THE THUMB IS IN CONTACT WITH THE NECK.

THE EXACT POSITION OF THE THUMB VARIES WITH EACH PLAYER, DEPENDING ON THE SHAPE OF HIS HAND. BUT IF THE VIOLIN HOLD IS SECURE, SO THAT THE THUMB DOES NOT FEEL THE NEED TO SUPPORT THE NECK, IT WILL FIND ITS OWN NATURAL POSITION. (See p.28). NOW LIFT THE BASE JOINT OF THE FIRST FINGER—*HEAR*, *SAY*, AND *FEEL* THE 'A' IN YOUR MIND, SIMULTANEOUSLY AND AT THE SAME TIME TRANSFERRING THIS SENSATION TO THE FIRST BASE JOINT AS IF THEY WERE ONE AND THE SAME. DROP THE FINGER FROM THE BASE JOINT FORWARD, A WHOLE TONE DISTANCE FROM THE NUT ON THE "G" STRING, TRY TO IMAGINE THAT 'A' SO STRONGLY IN THE BASE JOINT THAT EVEN WHEN THE FINGER-TIP IS IN CONTACT WITH THE STRING, IT FEELS AS IF THE BASE JOINT WERE HELD BACK BY THE ENERGY AND WEIGHT OF THE 'A'. THAT IS, WHILE THE FINGER IS ON THE STRING, THE GENERATING POWER ITSELF REMAINS BEHIND IN THE BONE OF

THE BASE JOINT, SO THAT THE ACTUAL CONTACT BETWEEN THE FINGER-TIP AND STRING IS LIGHT AND RESILIENT. REPEAT THIS SIX TIMES. STOP AND REST.

It may be difficult to keep the left wrist loose at first during this exercise. The best way to counter-act any possible stiffness is to 'buckle' the wrist very slightly towards you, after each finger-action on the string. By 'buckling' I mean a slight giving in of the wrist. This is an important addition to the exercises because it will ensure flexibility for the later, more difficult, and eventually virtuoso technique and should be practised by even those people whose wrists are loose by nature.

REPEAT EXERCISES 22 TO 27 STEP BY STEP MAKING SURE OF EVERY POINT. REPEAT EXERCISE 28 TWELVE TIMES AGAIN, BUT AFTER EACH CONTACT WITH THE STRING 'BUCKLE' THE WRIST FORWARD UNDER THE NECK.

EXERCISE 29

NOW TRY THE 'A' WITH THE BOW-STROKE.

CHECK ON *STANCE, VIOLIN-HOLD, BOW-HOLD.* HEAR AND SAY AND FEEL THE 'A' IN YOUR MIND RELATING IT TO THE BASE JOINT THROW THE FINGER FROM THE BASE JOINT FORWARD ONTO THE STRING CREATING A CIRCLE WITH THE THUMB. 'BUCKLE' THE WRIST. CHECK ON THE FLOATING POSITION OF THE RIGHT FORE-ARM AND THEN LET THE DOWN-STROKE OPEN FROM THE UPPER-ARM, IN A FORWARD MOTION UNTIL THE ARM IS COMPLETELY STRAIGHT. 'SCOOP' THE UPPER-ARM INWARDS TO RETURN WITH THE UP-STROKE DROPPING THE ELBOW AND FLEXING THE WRIST UNTIL THE FORE-ARM HAS RETURNED TO THE ORIGINAL 'FLOAT-ING POSITION'. KEEP THE CIRCLE BETWEEN THE INDEX FINGER AND THE THUMB IN THE LEFT HAND, AND ADJUST THE 'A' IF NEC-ESSARY. 'BUCKLE' THE WRIST AGAIN. REPEAT THIS VERY SLOWLY FOUR TIMES. STOP AND REST.

If the sound is not clear and true, adjust the weight of the base joint and make certain that the finger itself is always placed on its very tip. Make certain, too, that the finger action is forward and not twisted.

REPEAT THE ABOVE EXERCISE VERY SLOWLY FOUR TIMES. GO OVER EXERCISES 22 TO 28, THEN REPEAT EXERCISE 29 AGAIN.

BETWEEN LESSONS PRACTISE ONLY EXERCISES 23 TO 27.

NOTE TO ADVANCED PLAYERS

The cause of many technical frustrations, "violinistic neuroses," and physical tension is in a faulty vibrato. (See A NEW APPROACH to VIOLIN PLAYING p.10).

The trouble is that people are apt to think they are loosening their hand with a continuous vibrato while in fact very often they are stiffening it. The vibrato can become such a nervous habit that sometimes the player is unable to play a note without shaking his hand; and how could a continuously shaking hand remain loose during fast runs, shifts, double stops, etc. But as the break-down occurs mostly during fast runs (and not in the deceptively sweet-sounding slow passages), the cause of it is hardly ever attributed to a faulty vibrato.

Now of course a vibrato is necessary to give life and warmth to the tone, but it should be a natural development of the fundamental play-actions and not a super-imposed oscillation. That is why the above exercises are so essential because they deal with the fundamental play-actions; and when they are correctly applied there is an exciting, spontaneous vibrato in the tone. The player should stop his own vibrato during these exercises otherwise the natural vibrato will not be able to develop with the basic play-actions.

LESSON VI

CONSOLIDATION OF THE 1ST FINGER ACTION

Before going any further, please summarise the major points again.

1. *THE SEE-SAW IMAGE.* (p.3).
2. *THE STANCE.* (p.4).
3. *THE VIOLIN HOLD.* (p.5).
4. *THE BOW-HOLD* (p. 6).
5. *THE DOWN-STROKE.* (p.11).
6. *THE UP-STROKE.* (p.12).
7. *THE 'CIRCLE' BETWEEN LEFT THUMB AND INDEX FINGER.* (p.27).
8. *THE 'FORWARD' FINGER ACTION.* (p.29).
9. *THE FUNDAMENTAL BALANCES OF THE BASE JOINTS.* (p. 30, 31, 32).
10. *REPEAT EXERCISES 22 TO 29 IN LESSON V.*

EXERCISE 30

DURING EACH BAR OF PAUSE IN THE FOLLOWING EXERCISE, *HEAR, SAY* AND *FEEL* THE 'A' RELATING IT TO THE 1ST BASE JOINT. CHECK ON THE CIRCLE BETWEEN BASE JOINT AND THUMB, AND ON THE *FORWARD* ACTION OF THE BASE JOINT. ADJUST 'A' IF NECESSARY. BUCKLE LEFT WRIST GENTLY WHILE PLAYING THE 'A' DURING BOTH THE DOWN AND THE UP-STROKES.

STOP AND REST.

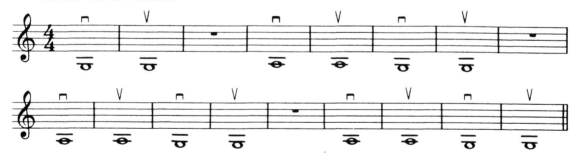

EXERCISE 31

FIND AN 'E' ON THE PIANO OR PLUCK THE OPEN STRING ON THE VIOLIN. LISTEN TO IT CAREFULLY FIRST, THEN SING IT. IF YOU USE THE OPEN E STRING AS A GUIDE, SING IT AN OCTAVE LOWER. AGAIN, DO NOT SAY 'LA' OR 'MM', BUT SAY THE 'E' WHILE YOU SING IT. THEN REPEAT EXERCISES 24 TO 29, BUT REPLACING THE 'A' WITH AN 'E' ON THE D STRING EVERY TIME WITH THE FIRST FINGER.

EXERCISE 32

DURING EACH BAR OF PAUSE, AS BEFORE WITH THE 'A', *HEAR*, *SAY*, AND *FEEL* THE 'E' THIS TIME, CONNECTING IT WITH THE FIRST BASE JOINT. CHECK ON THE CIRCLE BETWEEN BASE JOINT AND THUMB, AND ON THE FORWARD ACTION OF THE BASE JOINT. ADJUST THE 'E' IF NECESSARY. BUCKLE WRIST GENTLY WHILE PLAYING THE 'E' DURING BOTH THE DOWN AND THE UP-STROKES.

EXERCISE 33

NOW FIND THE 'B' ON THE PIANO. LISTEN TO IT CAREFULLY FIRST, THEN SING IT. IF THERE IS NO PIANO AVAILABLE, SING THE 'G' AND 'A' SIX TIMES IN SUCCESSION, OR UNTIL YOU GET USED TO HEARING THE TONE INTERVAL: THEN THE 'D' AND THE 'E'. PLAY THE OPEN STRING, THINK OF THE TONE INTERVAL, THEN SING THE 'B'. REPEAT THIS SIX TIMES. IF IT SEEMS DIFFICULT TO SING THE 'B', GO BACK TO SINGING THE 'G' AND 'A' SIX TIMES AND THE 'D' AND 'E' SIX TIMES AND THEN TRY THE 'A' AND 'B' AGAIN. IT SHOULD BE EASIER AND EASIER TO FIND EACH TIME YOU TRY. PLEASE ALWAYS SAY THE *NAME* OF EACH NOTE WHILE SINGING IT.

REPEAT EXERCISES 24 TO 29 IN LESSON V BUT REPLACING THE FIRST FINGER 'A' ON THE 'G' STRING WITH THE FIRST FINGER 'B' ON THE 'A' STRING EVERY TIME.

LEFT THUMB

Before going on to the following exercise, it is worth noting that because the A string is considerably nearer to the fingers than the G and D strings were, the tip of the thumb level on the other side of the neck may want to get as high or perhaps even higher than the top of the finger-board, in order to balance the forward action of the first finger. It is important to remember that the thumb is never used as a prop. It is a mobile point of balance in continuous movement; its position depending on which finger and string the player is using. If the violin-hold is secure, if the hand is straight with a loose wrist and a forward finger action, the thumb will always find its natural position. Watch a good player and see how alive and mobile his thumb is during rapid and difficult technical passages.

EXERCISE 34

DURING EACH BAR OF PAUSE, AS IN THE PREVIOUS EXERCISES, *HEAR*, *SAY* AND *FEEL* THE 'B' CONNECTING IT WITH THE FIRST BASE JOINT. CHECK ON THE CIRCLE BETWEEN THE BASE JOINT AND THE

THUMB, AND ON THE FORWARD ACTION OF THE BASE JOINT. ADJUST THE 'B' IF NECESSARY, BUCKLE LEFT WRIST GENTLY WHILE PLAYING THE 'B' DURING BOTH THE DOWN AND UP-STROKES. PLEASE REMEMBER TO LOWER YOUR RIGHT UPPER-ARM TO THE CORRECT LEVEL FOR THE 'A' STRING.

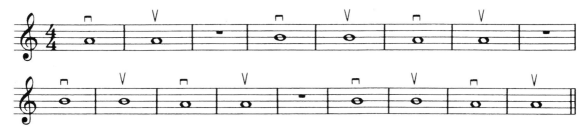

EXERCISE 35

FIND THE F♯ ABOVE THE OPEN E ON THE PIANO. LISTEN TO IT CAREFULLY THEN SING IT. IF THERE IS NO PIANO AVAILABLE, PLAY THE OPEN E STRING, SING IT, THEN SING A TONE INTERVAL FROM IT AND YOU WILL HAVE F♯. IF THIS SEEMS DIFFICULT IN THE BEGINNING, GO BACK AGAIN TO SINGING THE 'G' AND 'A' SIX TIMES AND THE 'D' AND 'E' SIX TIMES AS BEFORE. THEN TRY THE 'E' AND 'F♯' AGAIN. PLEASE REMEMBER TO SAY THE *NAME* OF EACH NOTE WHILE SINGING IT. REPEAT EXERCISES 24 TO 29. BUT *SUPPLEMENT* THE FIRST FINGER 'A' ON THE G STRING WITH THE FIRST FINGER 'F♯' ON THE 'E' STRING EVERY TIME.

Because of the nearness of the E string to the first base joint, there is a tendency to feel hampered there, and a cramped first finger is the result. The best cure for this is to exaggerate the lift and the *forward* motion of the first base joint, which will assure the freedom of its action. Make certain that there is no twist in the hand and that the left thumb is free and loose; because again, the tip of the thumb level may want to get even higher above the level of the finger-board than it did when you were playing on the A string.

EXERCISE 36

AGAIN, AS IN THE PREVIOUS EXERCISES, *HEAR*, *FEEL* AND *SAY* THE 'F♯' CONNECTING IT WITH THE FIRST BASE JOINT, DURING EACH BAR OF PAUSE. ADJUST THE F♯ IF NECESSARY. BUCKLE THE WRIST GENTLY WHILE PLAYING THE F♯ DURING BOTH THE DOWN AND THE UPSTROKE. CHECK ON THE CIRCLE BETWEEN BASE JOINT AND THUMB, AND ON THE FORWARD ACTION OF THE BASE JOINT. REMEMBER THAT, TO FIND THE RIGHT POISE FOR THE 'E' STRING YOUR RIGHT UPPER-ARM MUST BE DROPPED QUITE LOW, ALMOST NEXT TO YOUR BODY.

EXERCISE 37

SING THE TONE INTERVALS SIX TIMES BETWEEN THE 'G' AND 'A', SIX TIMES BETWEEN THE 'D' AND 'E', SIX TIMES BETWEEN THE 'A' AND 'B' AND SIX TIMES BETWEEN THE 'E' AND 'F♯'. NOW HALVE THE INTERVAL IN YOUR MIND BETWEEN THE 'E' AND 'F♯' AND YOU WILL FIND THE 'F♮'.

SING THE SEMITONE INTERVAL BETWEEN THE 'E' AND 'F♮' SIX TIMES. REPEAT EXERCISES 24 TO 29 IN LESSON V BUT INSTEAD OF PLAYING THE 'A' ON THE 'G' STRING REPLACE IT WITH THE SEMITONE 'F♮' ON THE 'E' STRING EVERYTIME.

This 'F♮' is right next to the nut, but make certain when playing it that you are *not pulling the finger backwards*—but that you exaggerate the lift of the first finger base-joint even more than when playing the 'F♯', so that the 'F♮' becomes a forward action too, in spite of its proximity to the nut.

EXERCISE 38

CHECK ON THE CIRCLE BETWEEN BASE JOINT AND THUMB AND ON THE FORWARD ACTION OF THE BASE JOINT. AGAIN, AS IN THE PREVIOUS EXERCISES, *HEAR, SAY* AND *FEEL* THE 'F♮' DURING EACH BAR OF PAUSE CONNECTING IT WITH THE FIRST BASE JOINT. BUCKLE THE LEFT WRIST GENTLY WHILE PLAYING THE 'F' DURING THE DOWN AND UP-STROKES. REMEMBER THAT ON THE E STRING YOUR RIGHT UPPER-ARM IS DROPPED QUITE LOW, ALMOST NEXT TO YOUR BODY TO FIND THE RIGHT POISE FOR THIS STRING.

EXERCISE 39

DURING THE RESTS, WHILE LIFTING THE BASE JOINT TO PREPARE THE 'F' OR 'F♯', LIFT THE BOW AS WELL, AND GET READY FOR ANOTHER DOWN-STROKE.

GREENSLEEVES

PLEASE PRACTISE ONLY *SINGING* THE INTERVALS IN LESSONS 30 TO 39 UNTIL YOUR NEXT LESSON.

NOTE TO ADVANCED PLAYERS

After going over these exercises thoroughly go over Lessons VII, VIII and IX and Exercises 1, 2, 3; in A NEW APPROACH TO VIOLIN PLAYING. (p.34).

LESSON VII

THE ANTICIPATION OF EACH NOTE

Before going on to the new exercises in this lesson please summarize the major points again.

1. *THE SEE-SAW IMAGE.* (p.3).
2. *THE STANCE.* (p.4).
3. *THE VIOLIN-HOLD.* (p.5).
4. *THE BOW-HOLD.* (p. 6).
5. *THE DOWN-STROKE.* (p.11).
6. *THE UP-STROKE.* (p.12).
7. *THE CIRCLE BETWEEN LEFT THUMB AND INDEX FINGER.* (p.27).
8. *THE FORWARD FINGER ACTION.* (p.29).
9. *THE FUNDAMENTAL BALANCES OF THE BASE JOINTS.* (p. 30, 31, 32)
10. *REPEAT EXERCISES 22 TO 29 IN LESSON V.*

EXERCISE 40

FIRST SING THE FOLLOWING EXERCISE NAMING EACH NOTE BY ITS PROPER NAME. THEN GO OVER IT AGAIN SILENTLY BUT *HEAR* EACH NOTE. NOW REPEAT IT ON THE VIOLIN BUT *HEAR, SAY* AND *FEEL* EACH 'A' CONNECTING IT WITH THE BASE JOINT LONG BEFORE THE 'G' STROKE IS ACTUALLY FINISHED. ADJUST EACH 'A' AND 'BUCKLE' THE WRIST. MAKE CERTAIN THAT IT IS THE *VERY* TIP OF THE FINGER THAT LANDS ON THE STRING.

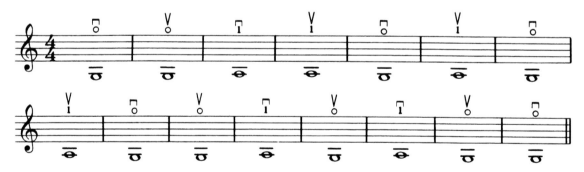

EXERCISE 41

SING IT. *HEAR, SAY* AND *FEEL* EACH 'E', RELATING IT TO THE BASE JOINT LONG BEFORE THE 'D' STROKE IS ACTUALLY FINISHED. ADJUST EACH 'E' AND MAKE CERTAIN THAT IT IS THE VERY TIP OF THE FINGER THAT LANDS ON THE STRING.

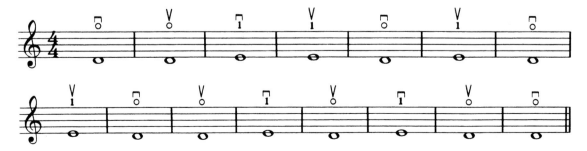

EXERCISE 42

SING IT. *HEAR, SAY* AND *FEEL* EACH 'B', RELATING IT TO THE BASE JOINT LONG BEFORE THE ACTUAL 'A' STROKE IS FINISHED. ADJUST EACH 'B'. BUCKLE THE LEFT WRIST. MAKE CERTAIN THAT IT IS THE VERY TIP OF THE FINGER THAT LANDS ON THE STRING.

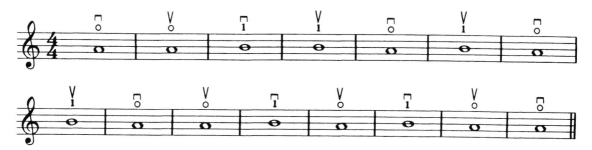

EXERCISE 43

SING IT. *HEAR, SAY* AND *FEEL* EACH 'F♮' AND 'F♯' LONG BEFORE THE 'E' STROKE IS FINISHED. REMEMBER TO EXAGGERATE THE LIFT OF THE FIRST FINGER BASE JOINT AND THE *FORWARD* MOTION OF THE FINGER ACTION WHEN PLAYING THE 'F♯' OR THE 'F♮'. REMEMBER CORRECT RIGHT ARM POSITION. MAKE CERTAIN LEFT THUMB IS LOOSE IN CASE IT WANTS TO ADJUST ITS POSITION.

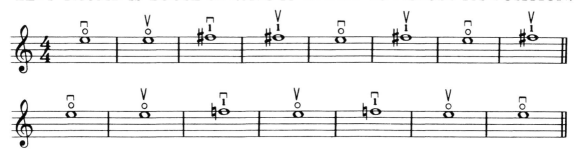

After the 'A' with the first finger on the 'G' string comes the 2nd finger 'B'. If you sing the 'A' again and then sing the next note a tone higher you will find the 'B'.

EXERCISE 44

PUT DOWN THE VIOLIN.

DROP YOUR LEFT ARM NEXT TO YOUR BODY WITH THE PALM FACING YOUR SIDE. STRAIGHTEN THE SECOND FINGER FROM THE BASE JOINT. AND JUST AS YOU HAVE DONE WITH THE FIRST FINGER 'A', IMAGINE THAT THE *SOUND*, THE *NAME* AND THE *FEELING* OF THAT 'B' ARE ONE AND THE SAME INHABITING THE BONE OF THE 2ND BASE JOINT, REPEAT THIS TWELVE TIMES.

SUSPEND YOUR LEFT ARM AS IF PLAYING THE VIOLIN. LET YOUR FINGERS CURL NATURALLY IN THE SHAPE OF THE DESCENDING STAIRCASE. LIFT THE 2ND FINGER FROM THE BASE JOINT AND AGAIN *HEAR, SAY* AND *FEEL* THE 'B' LODGED THERE SO STRONGLY THAT EVEN WHILE THE FINGER ITSELF IS THROWN *FORWARD* YOU FEEL THAT THE 'B' WITH ALL ITS ENERGY REMAINS BEHIND IN THE BASE JOINT.

DESCENDING INTERVALS

It is always much more difficult to prepare a descending interval on the violin than to prepare an ascending one, because it is more difficult to raise a finger which is underneath the previous one. So the preparation of the descending intervals demands special attention. It can not be underlined enough how important it is to learn to prepare *each* note on the violin from the very beginning regardless of whether the note happens to be above or below the previous one. The preparation of each note will assure a precise articulation, which is an invaluable asset to good music making, especially when playing Bach, Haydn and Mozart. Special care with the descending intervals will avoid the tendency of 'falling into' the notes below, creating finally an untidy effect in the fast passages.

If the note that follows is with the same finger, obviously the finger cannot be raised between the sounds. In this case, there should be an 'imaginary' lift in the base joint.

Put your left finger-tips on the back of your right hand as if you were playing the piano. Lift and drop your index finger. Then leave the finger down and feel an imaginary hammer-like action in the base joint, that is—a 'lift' and 'drop'. This will not be a visible action, but it will transmit to the finger-tip a slight, sensitive and mobile pulsation which you may feel on the skin of the other hand. And this is the kind of 'touch' you want on the string, when repeating the same note.

EXERCISE 45

FIRST SING THE FOLLOWING EXERCISE, AND ONLY THEN PLAY IT ON THE VIOLIN.

RAISE EACH BASE JOINT WITH THE *FEEL* OF THE NOTE IN IT LONG BEFORE THE STROKE OF THE PREVIOUS NOTE IS FINISHED. PAY SPECIAL ATTENTION TO THE DESCENDING INTERVAL—THAT IS, OF EACH 'A' WHICH COMES AFTER 'B', AND MAKE CERTAIN TO LIFT THE FIRST FINGER THAT IS ON THE NOTE 'A' AGAIN AS SOON AS THE FOLLOWING NOTE BEGINS.

After the 'E' with the first finger on the D string comes the 2nd finger 'F'. Please remember that the 'F' is only a *semi-tone* higher than the 'E'. So the 2nd finger is close on top of the 1st finger this time. Sing the 'E', then sing the note immediately above and you will find the 'F'.

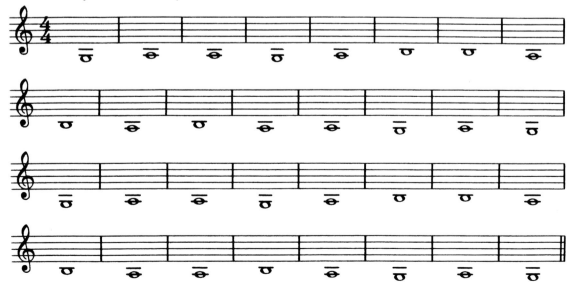

EXERCISE 46

AGAIN SING THE FOLLOWING EXERCISE FIRST, GIVING EACH NOTE ITS PROPER NAME, AND ONLY THEN PLAY IT ON THE VIOLIN. REMEMBER TO PREPARE EACH NOTE LONG BEFORE THE STROKE OF THE PREVIOUS NOTE IS FINISHED, PAYING SPECIAL ATTENTION TO THE DESCENDING INTERVAL. LIFT THE FIRST FINGER AGAIN AS SOON AS THE FOLLOWING NOTE BEGINS. REMEMBER THAT EACH FINGER ACTION IS A *FORWARD* MOTION ON THE FINGERBOARD. NEVER TWIST THE ARM OR HAND.

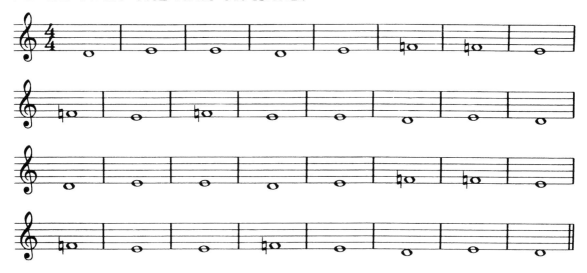

The 'F♯' on the D string with the second finger is a tone higher than the 'E' so there is space between the 1st and 2nd fingers this time. Sing 'E', 'F♮', and then 'E', 'F♯'.

EXERCISE 47

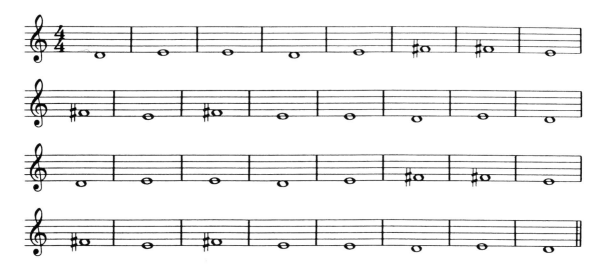

After the 'B' with the first finger on the 'A' string comes the 2nd finger 'C'. This is also only a semi-tone higher than the 'B' and so the second finger is close on top of the first finger on the A string too. Sing the 'A' and the 'B', then sing the next note adjacent to the 'B' and you will find the 'C♮'.

EXERCISE 48

SING THE FOLLOWING EXERCISE BEFORE PLAYING IT. REMEMBER TO PREPARE EACH NOTE LONG BEFORE THE STROKE OF THE PREVIOUS NOTE IS FINISHED, PAYING SPECIAL ATTENTION TO THE DESCENDING INTERVAL, AND TO LIFTING THE FIRST FINGER AGAIN AS SOON AS THE FOLLOWING NOTE BEGINS. REMEMBER TO ADJUST THE RIGHT UPPER-ARM TO THE CORRECT LEVEL FOR THE A STRING, AND THAT THE 'C' IS ONLY A *SEMI-TONE* HIGHER THAN THE 'B'.

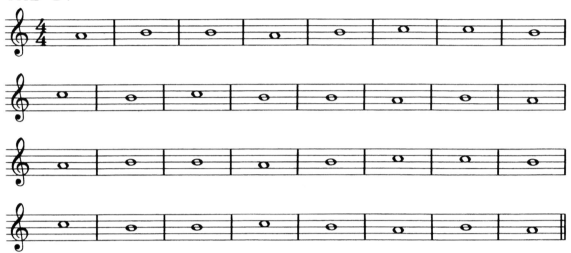

After the first finger 'F' which is right next to the nut on the E string, comes the 2nd finger 'G' a tone's distance away. Sing 'E', then 'F' and a tone higher is 'G'.

EXERCISE 49

SING THE FOLLOWING EXERCISE BEFORE PLAYING IT. REMEMBER TO PREPARE EACH NOTE LONG BEFORE THE STROKE OF THE PREVIOUS NOTE IS FINISHED. THIS SHOULD BE ESPECIALLY TRUE WHEN PLAYING A 1ST FINGER 'F♮' AFTER PLAYING A 2ND FINGER 'G'. MAKE CERTAIN BEFORE THE 'G' STROKE IS FINISHED THAT YOU RAISE THE BASE JOINT OF THE FIRST FINGER, AND THAT THE FINGER ACTION ITSELF IS A *FORWARD* MOTION IN SPITE OF ITS PROXIMITY TO THE NUT. NEVER PULL THE FINGER BACKWARDS IN A CROUCHING POSITION. REMEMBER TO ADJUST THE RIGHT UPPER-ARM TO THE CORRECT LEVEL FOR THE E STRING.

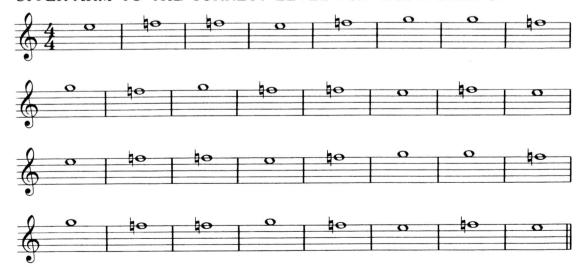

EXERCISE 50

GO OVER THE SAME POINTS AS IN THE PREVIOUS EXERCISE BUT THIS TIME PLAY 'F♯' ALL THE WAY THROUGH. REMEMBER THAT 'F♯' IS A TONE INTERVAL FROM THE NUT AND THE OPEN E STRING.

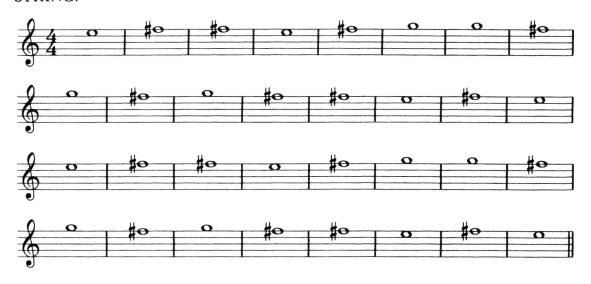

EXERCISE 51

PLAY THE OPEN G STRING, THEN THE 1ST FINGER 'A', SECOND FINGER 'B'. PUT DOWN THE 3RD FINGER PRACTICALLY ON TOP OF THE 'B' AND YOU HAVE THE 'C'—A SEMI-TONE DISTANCE FROM THE 'B'. SING IT SIX TIMES WITH ITS PROPER NAME.

PLAY THE OPEN D STRING THEN THE 1ST FINGER 'E', 2ND FINGER 'F' RIGHT ON TOP OF THE 'E'—SEMI-TONE DISTANCE. THEN PUT DOWN THE 3RD FINGER, A TONE AWAY, AND YOU HAVE THE 'G'. SING IT SIX TIMES WITH ITS PROPER NAME. (BUT MAKE CERTAIN NOT TO KEEP THE INTERMEDIATE FINGERS DOWN).

PLAY THE OPEN A STRING, THEN THE 1ST FINGER 'B' AND THE SECOND FINGER 'C' RIGHT ON TOP OF THE 'B', A SEMI-TONE DISTANCE. THEN PUT DOWN THE 3rd FINGER A TONE AWAY AND YOU HAVE THE 'D'. SING IT SIX TIMES WITH ITS PROPER NAME.

PLAY THE OPEN E STRING, THEN PUT THE 1ST FINGER 'F' RIGHT ON TOP OF THE NUT A SEMI-TONE DISTANCE AWAY, AND THE 2ND FINGER 'G' A TONE AWAY. PUT DOWN THE 3RD FINGER ALSO A TONE AWAY, AND YOU HAVE THE 'A'. SING THIS SIX TIMES WITH ITS PROPER NAME.

SING THE FOLLOWING EXERCISE NAMING EACH NOTE BY ITS PROPER NAME BEFORE PLAYING IT. PREPARE EACH FINGER FROM ITS BASE JOINT BEFORE THE PREVIOUS STROKE IS FINISHED, REGARDLESS OF WHETHER THE INTERVAL IS AN ASCENDING OR A DESCENDING ONE. MAKE CERTAIN THAT THE SEMI-TONE INTERVALS ARE NOT MERELY NEXT TO EACH OTHER BUT THAT THEY ARE *ON TOP OF OR RIGHT UNDERNEATH* EACH OTHER.

IF YOU BECOME TIRED DURING THE FOLLOWING EXERCISE WAIT AWHILE AT EACH REST AND CONTINUE ONLY AFTER THE FATIGUE HAS GONE.

JOHN PEEL

PLEASE PRACTISE ONLY *SINGING* THE NOTES IN EXERCISE 50
BUT DO NOT PLAY THEM ON THE VIOLIN UNTIL YOUR NEXT LESSON.

LESSON VIII

THE FOURTH FINGER

Before going any further, please check on the major points again.
1. *THE STANCE.* (p.4).
2. *THE VIOLIN AND BOW-HOLD.* (p.5, 6).
3. *THE BOW-STROKES.* (p.11, 12).
4. *THE CIRCLE BETWEEN THE LEFT THUMB AND THE INDEX FINGER.* (p.27).
5. *THE FORWARD LEFT FINGER ACTION.* (p.29).
6. *THE FUNDAMENTAL BALANCES OF THE LEFT FINGER BASE JOINTS.* (p. 30, 31, 32)
7. *THE BALANCE OF THE LEFT THUMB.* (p.38).
8. *THE DESCENDING INTERVAL.* (p.44).
9. *REPEAT EXERCISES 40 TO 51 IN LESSON VII.*

EXERCISE 52

HANG YOUR LEFT ARM NEXT TO YOUR BODY WITH THE PALM FACING YOUR SIDE. GO OVER IN YOUR MIND THE THREE NOTES YOU HAVE LEARNED ON EACH STRING, BOTH FORWARDS AND BACKWARDS, SAYING THE NAME OF EACH NOTE *ALOUD* AND AT THE SAME TIME RAISING EACH APPROPRIATE FINGER FROM THE BASE JOINT.

GO OVER THESE FIRST WITH 'F' IN THE KEY OF C—THEN WITH 'F♯' IN THE KEY OF 'G'. MAKE CERTAIN THAT YOU KNOW IN BOTH KEYS EXACTLY WHICH TWO FINGERS FALL PRACTICALLY ON TOP OF EACH OTHER, MAKING THE SEMI-TONE INTERVALS.

EXERCISE 53

FIRST SING EACH OF THE FOLLOWING EXERCISES, KEEPING ACCURATE TIME AND GIVING EACH NOTE ITS PROPER NAME. THEN PLAY EACH EXERCISE THREE TIMES, PAUSING IN BETWEEN TO CHECK THE MAJOR POINTS OF THE BOW-STROKES AND THE ACTION OF THE LEFT BASE JOINTS. IF THE PRINCIPLE OF HOW TO PREPARE EACH NOTE IS WELL UNDERSTOOD, ABBREVIATE THE THOUGHT PROCESS BEFORE EACH FINGER ACTION TO—"RAISE", "THROW", "BUCKLE": "RAISE", "THROW", "BUCKLE" ETC.

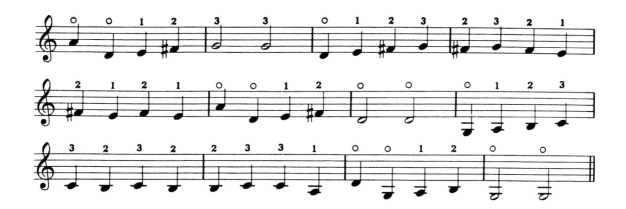

EXERCISE 54

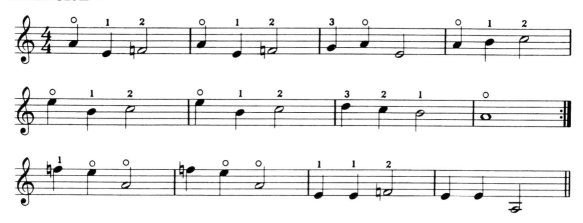

EXERCISE 55

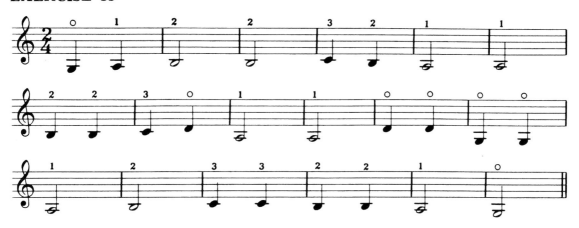

EXERCISE 56

EXERCISE 57

THE FOURTH FINGER

Stretch your left hand with the palm upwards and see what a considerable difference there is between the little finger and the three other fingers in length and width. The little finger is about the length of the thumb, but only about half as wide. This time there is no extra stretch between the third and fourth fingers, as there was between the thumb and the index finger. Also, as you will see, the little finger is not merely a point of balance as the thumb is in violin playing, but, alas, a very important and active factor in dealing with difficult passages which demand great strength, such as fingered octaves, tenths, etc. And as the little finger alone is unable to cope with these strenuous demands (which its adjective 'little' conveys rather pathetically) there is a tendency to abuse it by whipping it into action through sheer force. The feeling of stiffness akin to paralysis which often follows in the wake of this abuse, creates a state of anxiety so great that for many people it may destroy the whole of violin playing. So it must be stressed again most emphatically how vital it is to find, at the very beginning, the fundamental balance of this action, through which the demands made upon the little finger (in spite of its size and inherent weakness) leave it flexible and make its action effortless and completely secure.

Before going into a detailed explanation, I would like to point out again that any basic problem (such as the effortless action of the little finger) is the same, regardless of whether the player is a beginner or a virtuoso. The preparation and the training of it are exactly the same, and are equally important at all stages of violin playing. Only the natural facility and familiarity of dealing with the problem may differ.

Now in order to understand the point of balance here, let us go back to the see-saw image again, but this time in miniature.

Suspend your left arm as if playing the violin, with your fingers in the descending staircase position. Imagine that the pivot or centre of the see-saw is between the second finger and the thumb, and that the 1st finger represents one end of the plank, and the 3rd and 4th fingers the other end.

Illustration 31

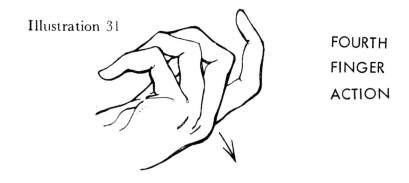

FOURTH
FINGER
ACTION

Now each time before using the 4th finger, tilt the base joint of the 1st finger *backwards* toward the scroll, as if it were the lower, heavier end of the plank. Then, relying on the strength and steadiness of this position, prepare the base joint of the 4th finger according to the exercises in Lessons V and VI. Throw the finger from the base joint lightly onto its place, a tone distant on each string from the 'third finger note' below it: a 'D' on the G string, an 'A' on the D string, 'E' on the A string, and 'B' on the E string. They are easy to check because apart from the 'B' on the E string, the other three can be tried out with the corresponding open strings.

Here, although the balance depends on the support of the first base joint, the function of the energy-generating 4th base joint, and the forward action of the finger from it, are more important than ever. But to achieve good results, you must make certain that all previous points, such as the stance, violin-hold, bow-hold, etc. are correct. Because violin playing, through this approach, is like a chain of links, each point of balance is interlocked and interdependent with another to create an effortless power of strength. But just as with a chain of links, if one is broken, the whole chain loses its sense of purpose.

Once this principle of the 4th finger action is understood, the release from tension is so liberating, that the music of composers like Paganini and Ernst becomes easy and enjoyable, as many an advanced player has discovered.

EXERCISE 58

DURING EACH BAR OF REST, PREPARE YOUR HAND FOR THE 4TH FINGER ACTION. (i) TILT THE BASE JOINT OF THE INDEX FINGER BACKWARDS TOWARDS THE SCROLL (THE HEAVY END OF THE SEE-SAW). (ii) POISE THE 4TH FINGER FROM THE BASE-JOINT ABOVE THE STRING (RELYING ON THE BALANCING WEIGHT OF THE FIRST FINGER). (iii) HEAR, SAY AND FEEL THE NOTE THERE, THEN THROW IT FROM THE BASE-JOINT ONTO ITS PLACE. ADJUST THE NOTE AND 'BUCKLE' THE WRIST. PLEASE REMEMBER TO RAISE EACH FINGER SLIGHTLY WHEN ITS BOW-STROKE IS FINISHED IN THE ASCENDING INTERVALS, SO THAT YOU CAN PREPARE IT AGAIN IN THE DESCENDING INTERVALS.

EXERCISE 59

THOUGH THERE IS NO ACTUAL REST IN THE FOLLOWING EXERCISE BEFORE THE 4TH FINGER ACTION, MAKE CERTAIN TO STOP LONG ENOUGH TO PREPARE IT CORRECTLY. THE EXTRA PREPARATION OF THE 4TH FINGER IS AN IMPORTANT POINT TO GET USED TO. IT WILL STAND YOU IN GOOD STEAD LATER ON WITH THE DOUBLE STOPS AND RAPID PASSAGES.

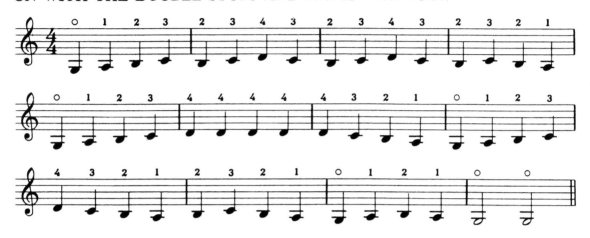

EXERCISE 60

EXERCISE 61

54

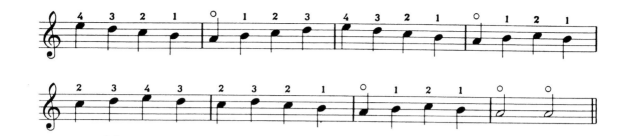

EXERCISE 62

ON TOP OF OLD SMOKY

THINK ABOUT THE 4*TH* FINGER ACTION, BUT DO NOT PRACTISE IT ON YOUR OWN.

LESSON IX

THE INTERMEDIATE FINGERS

Again, as before, please think over and check on the major points.

1. *THE STANCE.* (p.4).
   (a)   The Violin and Bow-hold.
   (b)   The Bow-strokes.
2. *THE FUNDAMENTAL BALANCES OF THE LEFT FINGER BASE*
   (a)   The 'Circle': the balance of the left thumb.   *JOINTS* (p. 30, 31, 32)
   (b)   The forward left finger action.
   (c)   The anticipation and preparation of *each* base joint, especially in the descending intervals.
3. *THE FOURTH FINGER ACTION.* (p.52).
4. *REPEAT EXERCISES 58 TO 62 IN LESSON VIII.*

EXERCISE 63

HANG YOUR LEFT ARM NEXT TO YOUR BODY WITH THE PALM FACING YOUR SIDE. GO OVER IN YOUR MIND THE FOUR NOTES ON EACH STRING (i.e. 'A' 'B' 'C' 'D' ON THE 'G' STRING) BOTH BACKWARDS AND FORWARDS SAYING THE NAME OF EACH NOTE *ALOUD* AND STRAIGHTENING AND "DROPPING" EACH APPROPRIATE FINGER FROM THE BASE JOINT.

GO OVER THESE EXERCISES FIRST WITH 'F♮' IN THE KEY OF C—THEN WITH F♯ IN THE KEY OF G. MAKE CERTAIN THAT YOU KNOW IN BOTH KEYS EXACTLY WHICH TWO FINGERS FOLLOW CLOSELY ON TOP OF EACH OTHER BECAUSE OF THE SEMI-TONE INTERVAL. THEN PLAY EACH OF THE FOLLOWING EXERCISES THREE TIMES.

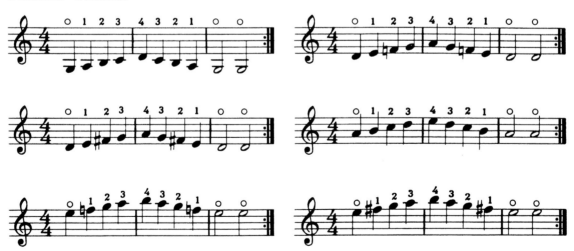

EXERCISE 64

HANG YOUR ARM NEXT TO YOUR BODY WITH THE PALM FACING YOUR SIDE. GO OVER IN YOUR MIND THE FOUR NOTES THAT ARE *OPPOSITE* EACH OTHER ON THE FOUR STRINGS (i.e. THE FIFTH

56

INTERVALS 'A' 'E' 'B' AND 'F') IMAGINING THE FOUR FINGERS ON THE STRINGS IN TURN. GO OVER THESE EXERCISES FIRST TOWARDS THE 'E' STRING THEN BACK TO THE G, SAYING THE NAMES OF EACH NOTE *ALOUD*, AT THE SAME TIME 'RAISING' AND 'THROWING' EACH APPROPRIATE FINGER FROM THE BASE JOINT.

GO OVER THESE EXERCISES FIRST WITH 'F' IN THE KEY OF 'C', THEN WITH 'F♯' IN THE KEY OF 'G'. MAKE CERTAIN THAT YOU KNOW THE DIFFERENCE IN INTERVAL AND POSITION BE-TWEEN THE 'B' AND 'F♮', AND BETWEEN THE 'B' AND 'F♯', FOR WHILE THE 'B' AND 'F♯' ARE OPPOSITE EACH OTHER, THE 'F♮' IS LOWER THAN THE 'B'. IT IS THE SAME WITH THE 'F♯' AND THE 'C'. PLAY THE FOLLOWING EXERCISES THREE TIMES: THEN THREE TIMES AGAIN WITH ONLY AN IMAGINARY LIFT IN THE BASE JOINT. (see p.44).

THE INTERMEDIATE FINGERS

When the intervals become varied, so that the fingers do not follow each other in tone and semi-tone succession—please learn to put your fingers on the intermediate notes between the intervals. (But raise them again as soon as you find the note you want). This is a most rewarding habit to cultivate in the beginning, because it develops a feeling of security which, as was said before, is the perfect antidote to anxiety.

It is important to realize that each finger action involves a subtle, delicate shift in the left hand balance, which depends on the succession and distance of intervals and string crossings. Of course, there cannot be any hard and fast rules about this, as everybody's hand is different in size and shape. But for example, as the 1st and 2nd finger actions are obviously heavier than the 3rd and the 4th, it is necessary to lighten their touch. So, when projecting your mental image of 'raise and throw', visualise the respective base joints as far back towards the scroll as possible; while the 3rd and 4th fingers, especially the 4th, are thrown from the tilted balance of the 1st.

Also, as we have seen before, the position of the whole hand is continually changing, even to the height of the left thumb-tip at the neck, depending on whether the notes are on the G, D, A or E strings.

This may sound complicated at first, but if you think it out, it is merely common sense if tension is to be avoided. And the principle behind it is that no finger action is ever rigid or mechanical, that each note has to be felt, sensed and created: 'wooed' as Kreisler has said, 'wooed like a woman'. But then, this is where the very essence of violin playing lies; in the excitement of continuous creation.

On the other hand, as you will see, once each separate fundamental balance is achieved, it will be gathered into one control, directed by the left finger action (from the base joint).

Let us take the bow-stroke as an example. Whereas the balance of the right arm creates a perfect entity while playing on the open strings, when it comes to the interval progression from one finger to another, it would be senseless to rush on regardless with the bow, unless the left finger action, according to the demands of the interval progression was ready to *receive* the stroke. And as the facility of the finger action is obviously varied according to the size of the interval and the preparation necessary for it, the bow-stroke must vary accordingly. But if the balances are right, and if the command of the left finger action is secure, the bow-stroke will instinctively respond, without the player having to give it a thought. Many an advanced player suffers considerable anxiety because of stumbling left fingers trying to catch up with the mechanical regularity of the bow-stroke.

The same goes for string crossing as well. If all the incidental noises are to be avoided (similar to those of an untidy soup-eater) the lead must be in the left finger action, so the bow responds to it. These may seem merely split second niceties, but they make all the difference in the world to a feeling of security and to good music making.

As for the change of bow: if the control of the melodic pattern is in the left hand action, the bow will stay poised at the end of each stroke like a swing, before the ensuing left finger action assures its new momentum. And the change will not only be smooth and musical (one of the major goals of all violinists) but the strokes will feel as if self-propelled.

EXERCISE 65

'RAISE' 'THROW' 'BUCKLE' ALL THE WAY THROUGH THE FOL-LOWING EXERCISES. MAKE CERTAIN TO PUT DOWN THE INTER-MEDIATE FINGERS ON THE STOPS WHEN NECESSARY, ESPECIALLY WHEN GOING FROM ONE STRING TO ANOTHER. BUT LIFT THEM AS SOON AS THE NOTE YOU PREPARED IS READY FOR THE BOW-STROKE. ADJUST EACH NOTE AND CHECK ON THE 'CIRCLE'.

EXERCISE 66

PLEASE STOP LONG ENOUGH BEFORE THE 4TH FINGER ACTION TO BUILD UP THE INTERMEDIATE NOTES. MAKE CERTAIN THAT THE 4TH FINGER ACTION IS A FORWARD MOTION. (SEE FOURTH FINGER ACTION). DO NOT TWIST THE HAND. SING THE EXERCISE FIRST AND THEN PLAY IT THREE TIMES ON THE VIOLIN.

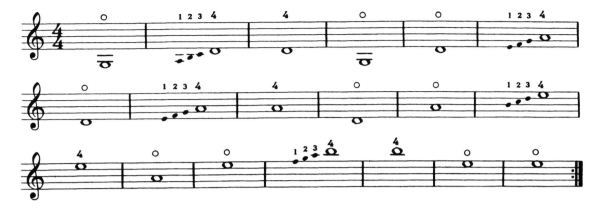

EXERCISE 67

SING IT FIRST, THEN 'RAISE' 'THROW' 'BUCKLE'

EXERCISE 68

 IS THE SYMBOL OF THE TIE WHICH MEANS THAT THE NOTES UNDER OR ABOVE IT ARE PLAYED WITH THE SAME STROKE.

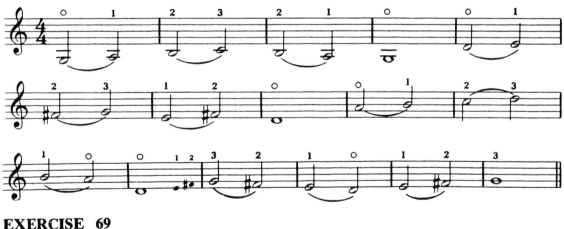

EXERCISE 69

EXERCISE 70

EXERCISE 71

EXERCISE 72

LONDONDERRY AIR

PRACTISE EXERCISES 63, 64 *WITHOUT* THE VIOLIN.

LESSON X

THE SCALES

Please go over and check on the major points again.
1. *THE STANCE.* (p.4).
   (a) The Violin and Bow-hold.
   (b) The Bow-stroke.
2. *THE FUNDAMENTAL BALANCES OF THE LEFT FINGER BASE*
   (a) The 'Circle': the balance of the left thumb.   *JOINTS.* (p. 30, 31, 32)
   (b) The forward left finger action.
   (c) The anticipation and preparation of *each* base joint, especially in the descending intervals.
3. *THE FOURTH FINGER ACTION.* (p.52).
4. *THE INTERMEDIATE FINGERS.* (p.57).
5. REPEAT EXERCISES **66, 67, 68, 69** IN LESSON IX.

EXERCISE 73

THE FOLLOWING EXERCISE WITH THE ♯s AND ♮s IS THE PRACTICE OF CHROMATIC, OR SEMI-TONE PROGRESSION ON EACH STRING. A NOTE WITH A FLAT IN FRONT OF IT BECOMES A SEMI-TONE LOWER; FOR EXAMPLE, THE 2ND FINGER 'B' ON THE G STRING WITH A FLAT IN FRONT OF IT BECOMES 'B♭' AND IS NOW ONLY A SEMI-TONE FROM THE FIRST FINGER A. AND A NOTE WITH A SHARP IN FRONT OF IT (AS WE HAVE SEEN WITH THE F♯) BECOMES A SEMI-TONE HIGHER PLAYED DIRECTLY UNDER THE NEIGHBOURING FINGER. SING EACH EXERCISE FIRST, SAYING THE NAME OF EACH NOTE AND ONLY THEN TRY IT ON THE VIOLIN. PLEASE DO NOT GROPE WITH THE FINGER-TIP BUT CONCENTRATE ON THE IMAGINARY LIFT OF THE BASE JOINTS. CHECK NOTES WITH OPEN STRINGS WHENEVER POSSIBLE TO MAKE CERTAIN YOU ARE IN TUNE.

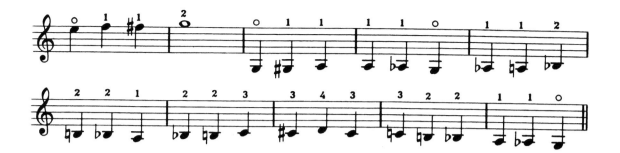

THE SCALES

If you look at any classical music and learn to analyse it (a most useful and at the same time fascinating pastime) you will find that the foundation of the most complex piece is often based on only a few notes from a certain scale. We all know the difference between major and minor scales; that while the major scale generally expresses something gay and cheerful, the minor scale is often used to express something sad or even tragic. But what is even more important to realize is that the scales are built on intervals, and that each interval has its own individual tonal colouring within the scale, (i.e. the major third, minor third etc.)

In order to do justice to all these differences, it is not enough to play each stop in tune by itself, but it is important to pitch each note according to the interval before and the interval following it, for example, an 'F♯' in E major (where it is the second note of the scale) has quite a different colouring from the 'F♯' in G Major where it is the all important seventh note.

This keen awareness of the delicate interval colouring is of course closely connected with ear training, the preparation of each note, and the continuous shift of balances in the left hand finger-action. (p. 57, 58). And to achieve any skill in this combination, a thorough knowledge of scales is indispensable. Unfortunately, because of the old mechanical process of 'finger strengthening', to some people, scales mean no more than boredom and drudgery. But if the scales are approached as the foundation of all music (which of course they *are*) this misconception no longer holds true. For the preparation and the creation of each note within a scale is just as exciting and as wholly absorbing as in any given piece—"That is why on the violin it is as difficult and as much evidence of control to draw one beautiful sound or to play one scale as it is to play a Concerto." Yehudi Menhuhin, (See Foreward in A NEW APPROACH TO VIOLIN PLAYING.)

During the preparation and creation of each note within the scale it is a good opportunity to say a few words about 'dynamics'—that is, the control of volume. If you want a loud sound, please *never press the stick with your finger*—but adjust the weight of your right upper-arm accordingly. For it is the degree of weight from the upper-arm transmitted (through the bent thumb *underneath* the stick) to the bow on the strings that controls the volume of tone.

But actually if all the fundamental balances are well established, the control of dynamics becomes a spontaneous action, as a natural part of your musical imagination.

The playing of scales is a continuous part of music-making and of every day routine. They can be practised in so many different ways and expanded to such a degree of virtuosity, that it is only possible here to present the four major scales up to four sharps and the four major scales up to four flats.

EXERCISE 74

SING EACH SCALE FIRST AND OBSERVE THE SHARPS AND FLATS AND THE SEMI-TONE FORMATIONS CAREFULLY. PLAY EACH SCALE AND THE ACCOMPANYING EXERCISE THREE TIMES. REST FREQUENTLY.

USE THE INTERMEDIATE NOTES WHEN NECESSARY. "RAISE" "THROW" "BUCKLE" AND ADJUST EACH NOTE.

PLEASE ONLY SING THE EXERCISES BETWEEN LESSONS.

G MAJOR

EXERCISE 75

D MAJOR

EXERCISE 76

A MAJOR

EXERCISE 77

E MAJOR

EXERCISE 78

F MAJOR

EXERCISE 79

B♭ MAJOR

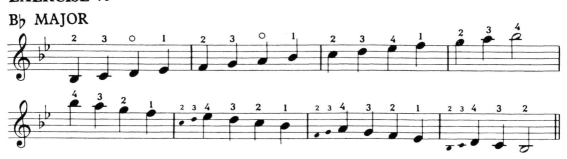

EXERCISE 80

E♭ MAJOR

EXERCISE 81

A♭ MAJOR

EXERCISE 82

C MAJOR

DRINK TO ME ONLY WITH THINE EYES

NOTE TO THE ADVANCED PLAYER

One of the most important aspects of this approach is that all technical problems are tackled through the medium of tone production, so it is an essential practice to make scales and arpeggios into music. Practice them slowly first with intense tone production (as if they were part of the 2nd movement of a Concerto) trying only three notes to a bow—then six—then twelve etc. It is most important not to play them suddenly fast but to increase the speed very gradually.

Wessely or Carl Flesch are most comprehensive, the latter being, of course, the most advanced. Exercises 3, 4 (In addition to 1, 2) in A NEW APPROACH TO VIOLIN PLAYING (pp.34, 35) are helpful preparations for the scales.

LESSON XI

THE BOWING TECHNIQUE
Please check on the major points again before going any further.
1. *THE STANCE*. **(p. 4).**
   (a) The Violin and Bow-hold.
   (b) The Bow-stroke.
2. *THE FUNDAMENTAL BALANCES OF THE LEFT FINGER BASE*
   (a) The 'Circle': the balance of the left thumb.   *JOINTS*. **(p. 30, 31, 32)**
   (b) The forward left finger action.
   (c) The anticipation and preparation of each base joint, especially in the descending intervals. **(p. 44).**
3. *THE FOURTH FINGER ACTION*. **(p.52).**
4. *THE INTERMEDIATE FINGERS*. **(p.57).**
5. REPEAT LESSON X.

THE BOWING TECHNIQUE
The 'Bowing Technique' is an impressive and well known phrase in any violinist's vocabulary. To the casual listener it merely conveys the idea of the bow flying across the strings with so much ease and speed in the hand of the virtuoso, that they are hardly aware of what is happening, apart from a cascade of sounds emanating from the flashing bow-hair. But alas, on looking closer, one tends to see it as an entity by itself locked up in learned books and accompanied by hundreds of exercises. To many a poor student, 'Bowing Technique' seems nothing less than a veritable labyrinth through which he hopefully tries to find a road.

Now no doubt there are many roads leading to Rome. But it is well worth thinking out which is the shortest and smoothest, and which gives the most assurance against breaking down or getting fatigued on the way. And as we have seen over and over again, only freedom from anxiety can guarantee complete assurance. Also as we have seen, this freedom from anxiety, as far as violin playing is concerned, depends entirely on an effortless control of movements. So we are back to the basic principle again—to the self-propelled play-actions of the fundamental balances.

Once this principle and the logic of its workings is really understood, bowing technique will cause no difficulty at all; because, though the length and speed will vary according to the strokes, it will all be governed by the same law as was the open string bowing. (see Lesson II p.10).

However, for a thorough understanding of the functions of the fundamental balances, it is most important to realize that in the long run, there are no such things as 'bowing technique', 'left hand technique' etc., but that good violin playing depends on the co-ordination of all the balances into a final 'whole'; and that the basic control of this 'whole' lies in the shaping of the melody in the left finger action. For it is through this that the precise articulation of the melodic progression is transmitted with its hundreds of variations.

So long as the basic play-action of the bowing arm is well established, the strokes are flexible and respond smoothly to the ever varying melodic progression indicated in the left hand.

In this lesson I shall deal only with the legato, Detaché and Martelé strokes, for these are possible to master at all stages of violin playing—as soon as the long bow-strokes are established. But as the playing of spiccato, staccato etc. demands a more dexterous left finger action than is normally possible for a beginner to achieve, I will not discuss them here. Teachers and advanced players who are following this book should turn to A NEW APPROACH TO VIOLIN PLAYING pp. 48, 49 and 53.

THE LEGATO

The legato (see Lesson IX) is an arch example of the necessity of establishing each fundamental balance separately at first, and then co-ordinating it into the play-action control of the left finger base joints. This is impossible unless the fundamental balances *are* well established. (See Lesson V).

The goal of the legato is a smooth progression of notes tied together on long relaxed strokes. So first of all, the bowing itself must be effortless, with smooth strokes and inaudible change of bow. (see Lesson II p.15). But this is one thing on the open strings, and another when the smoothness has to be achieved through "shifts", string crossings, and the multi-coloured tapestry of melodic progression. Obviously the duration of each bow-stroke is continuously changing, depending on the activity of the left fingers. So it is imperative that the right arm should follow the command of the left hand. In this way concentration need not be diffused (often a major cause for anxiety) but can be centralized at one focal point which can carry the responsibility of the whole, i.e. the fundamental balances of the left finger actions.

EXERCISE 83

1. SET THE RIGHT ARM FOR SLOW BOWING AS IF PLAYING ON THE OPEN STRINGS. THEN CONCENTRATE ONLY ON THE PROGRESSION OF THE LEFT FINGER BASE JOINTS.

2. PREPARE THE INTERMEDIATE NOTES WITHOUT STOPPING THE STROKES.

3. SEE WHAT A DIFFERENCE THERE IS IN THE LENGTH OF PREPARATION BETWEEN THE 'G' AND 'B' AND BETWEEN THE 'B' AND 'C' ETC. PAY SPECIAL ATTENTION TO THE PREPARATION OF THE DESCENDING INTERVALS.

PLAY THE G MAJOR SCALE (p.64) AND ONLY THEN PLAY THE FOLLOWING 2 EXERCISES.

EXERCISE 84

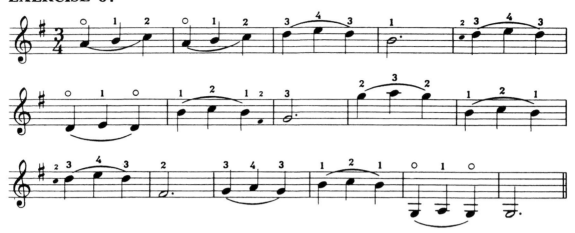

EXERCISE 85

PLAY THE A MAJOR SCALE (p.65). SING THE EXERCISE BEFORE
PLAYING IT. BE CAREFUL OF THE RHYTHM.

DETACHÉ

Detaché is a very commonly used bow-stroke. It means, literally, 'detached
strokes', that is, a stroke for each note, but, in effect, the resulting sounds are as
smooth as the legato.

The Detaché is generally in the upper half of the bow (from the middle to
the tip) and is generally a swift stroke in quavers or semi-quavers, and exactly the
same principle is applied to it as to the legato.

EXERCISE 86

ESTABLISH THE FUNDAMENTAL BALANCE OF THE BOWING ARM,
FOR THE STROKES ARE EXACTLY THE SAME AS YOU LEARNED IN
LESSON II, BUT ARE APPLIED ONLY IN THE *UPPER HALF OF THE
BOW*

EXERCISE 87

ESTABLISH THE FUNDAMENTAL BALANCES OF THE LEFT FINGER ACTION IN THE WAY YOU HAVE LEARNED IN LESSONS V, VI, VII AND VIII. CONCENTRATE ON THE INTERVAL PROGRESSION, PREPARING EACH NOTE, AND THE BOW WILL FOLLOW THE INEVITABLE FLUCTUATION OF THE LEFT FINGER ACTION. THIS WILL ACHIEVE A REASSURING 'MUSIC MAKING' QUALITY INSTEAD OF A MECHANICAL PROGRESSION. USE THE INTERMEDIATE NOTES. NOTE THE DIFFERENCES IN LENGTH OF PREPARATION BETWEEN THE LARGE AND SMALL INTERVALS. PAY SPECIAL ATTENTION TO THE DESCENDING INTERVALS. START THE EXERCISE IN THE MIDDLE OF THE BOW.

PLAY THE G MAJOR SCALE AND THEN REPEAT THE EXERCISE.

EXERCISE 88

IN THIS EXERCISE THE LENGTH OF THE BOW STROKE DEPENDS ON THE DEXTERITY OF THE LEFT FINGER ACTION. THE MORE FLUENT IT IS, THE SHORTER THE BOW STROKES BECOME, SIMPLY BECAUSE THERE WILL BE NO TIME FOR LONG STROKES. WHEN THE STROKES DECREASE IN LENGTH, YOU WILL FIND IT EASIER AND MORE NATURAL TO STAY NEARER THE MIDDLE THAN THE TIP OF THE BOW.

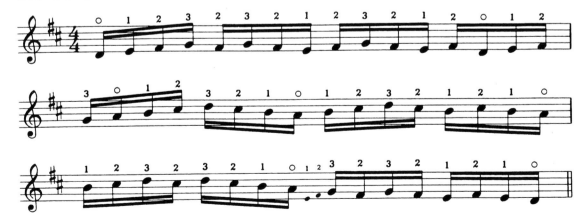

PLAY THE D MAJOR SCALE, AND THEN REPEAT THE EXERCISE.

MARTELÉ

The Martelé is a short, sharp stroke with a space between each sound. It is generally played in quavers, or in semi-quavers, with the upper part of the bow, but in fast tempo only at the tip. The Martelé is indicated by a dot above or below each note. It is an important stroke, especially in the festive, exuberant passages of Bach or Handel. With the Martelé, almost more than with any other bowing, it is important for the stroke to be nothing more than the tail-end of the right arm movement riding on the momentum of the 'throw' and 'scoop' of the upper arm, and from the overall control of the motivating power in the back. (See Lessons II and III). Never, never tear the strokes from the fore-arm, for not only will that create a harsh sound, but the arm will become stiff in no time, too.

EXERCISE 89

PLACE THE MIDDLE OF THE BOW ON THE STRING. ESTABLISH THE FEELING OF WEIGHT IN THE BACK AND, WITH THE SWIFTEST MOVEMENT POSSIBLE, 'THROW' THE UPPER ARM FORWARD SO THAT THE ARM IS STRETCHED WHEN THE BOW IS PLAYING AT THE TIP. THE SWIFTER THE THROW, THE SHARPER THE SOUND, BECAUSE OF THE ABRUPTNESS OF THE MOVEMENT. IT ALSO ASSURES A SUDDEN STOP OF THE BOW, WHICH IS SO IMPORTANT FOR THE SPACES BETWEEN THE NOTES. THEN JUST AS SWIFTLY SLAM THE UPPER ARM AND ELBOW DOWN NEXT TO YOUR BODY (AS IF PLAYING A BAGPIPE) WHICH ENSURES A SHARP EFFORTLESS UP-STROKE WITH THE SAME ABRUPT STOP AS BEFORE. PAY SPECIAL ATTENTION TO THE SPACES BETWEEN THE NOTES, AND MAKE CERTAIN TO STOP LONG ENOUGH TO THINK OUT THE ENSUING STROKE *BEFORE* PLAYING IT.

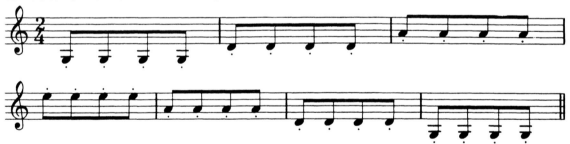

EXERCISE 90

ONCE THE FEELING OF THIS STROKE IS MASTERED, CONCENTRATE ONLY ON THE LEFT HAND, FOR THE FINAL CONTROL IS ALWAYS THERE. USE THE INTERMEDIATE NOTES. NOTE THE DIFFERENCES IN THE LENGTH OF PREPARATION BETWEEN THE LARGE AND SMALL INTERVALS. PAY SPECIAL ATTENTION TO THE PREPARATION OF THE 4TH FINGER. MAKE CERTAIN TO ADJUST THE UPPER ARM TO THE LEVEL OF EACH STRING.

EXERCISE 91
MAKE CERTAIN THAT THE STRING CROSSING IS FROM THE UPPER ARM, AND NOT ONLY FROM THE WRIST AND HAND.

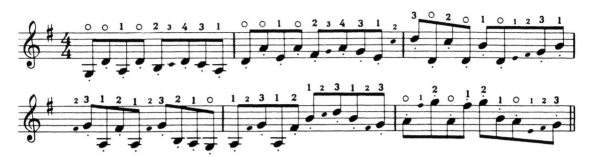

DOUBLE STOPS

The playing of double stops is one of the most exciting and most satisfying parts of violin playing. For only through the playing of double stops and chords is the violin completely liberated from dependence on any other instrument or instruments, such as a piano, another violin, orchestra, etc. How well one knows the familiar plea from kind relatives and friends, who have heard that you are learning the violin, "Play something for us" and the panicky answer "I cannot possibly without an accompanist."

The truth of the matter is, that though violin playing is very close to singing, one feels rather exposed standing up and playing a melody alone. To do this takes rather a special kind of talent, and apart from a few gypsies, the only person whom I ever knew who was able to do it at the drop of a hat, was Laurie Lee, the poet.

But if one is at ease with the double stops and chords, a whole new world of possibilities opens up, including the Bach solo sonatas, Paganini études etc. Also one gains a wonderful feeling of musical power, created by this complete independence from any other instrument.

Again—it is most important to realize that there is no 'elementary' and 'advanced' way of playing double stops. The approach is always the same, differing only in the actual level of execution. If the double stops are properly played, so that they never entail any struggle or strain, the beginner can have just as much enjoyment out of them as does the advanced player.

But of course stiffness in the left hand, a well known complaint when the fingers are stretched in all directions, is more apparent when playing double stops than when playing anything else. And in order to avoid this, it is imperative that each point of balance you have learned so far should be interlocked with and interdependent of every other. For example, unless the violin-hold is correct, the left arm cannot be free, and if the left arm is twisted, the left finger action is cramped, or, if the finger action is twisted, the wrist gets stiff, and if the control of finger-action is not from the base joints, the thumb gets disabled etc., etc. As it is impossible to enjoy double stops unless all these points are right, please check on all of them again before going any further.

One of the most important points is, always to concentrate on the lower finger first, not necessarily the lower sounding one, but the lower in position. We have seen with the 4th finger before, that it is thrown from the balance of the backward tilted index finger. And as the 4th finger is an important asset in double stops, make certain to apply this principle all the time. This continuous backward tilt also assures a correct wrist position with the fingers above their stops. (See 4th finger action p.52).

73

As for the bowing arm, do not try to place the bow on two strings at the same time, for the right hand will (out of sheer anxiety) immediately want to press into the stick. Place the bow, with upper-arm at the correct level for the lower sounding string only (such as the G when playing on the G, and D) because the curve of the bridge slopes toward the right anyhow, so nothing could be easier than to touch the higher sounding string with the curve of the stroke.

EXERCISE 92

PLACE THE BOW, WITH THE UPPER-ARM AT THE CORRECT LEVEL FOR THE LOWER SOUNDING STRING, AND WITH THE UP-BOW STROKE TIP THE STICK SLIGHTLY WITH THE LITTLE FINGER TOWARDS THE HIGHER SOUNDING STRING—BUT THE LEVEL OF THE UPPER-ARM SHOULD NOT CHANGE.

MAKE CERTAIN OF THE 'CIRCLE' IN THE LEFT HAND AND THE 'FORWARD' FINGER ACTION. 'PREPARE', 'THROW', 'BUCKLE' AND MAKE CERTAIN THAT THE BASE JOINT OF THE LOWER FINGER RETAINS THE GENERATING POWER.

PLAY THIS EXERCISE VERY SLOWLY. PAY CAREFUL ATTENTION TO THE DIFFERENCE BETWEEN THE TONE AND SEMI-TONE INTERVALS. 'BUCKLE' YOUR LEFT WRIST FREQUENTLY TO AVOID STIFFNESS. IF THE DOUBLE STOP USE AN OPEN STRING, PLAY THE OPEN STRING FIRST AND THEN THE OTHER NOTE. OTHERWISE PLEASE PLAY THE NOTE WITH THE LOWER FINGER FIRST.
USE ONLY HALF A BOW FOR THE QUAVERS WHICH ARE NOT TIED.
BEGIN IN THE LOWER HALF.

EXERCISE 93

EXERCISE 94

GREEN GROW THE RUSHES O

USE WHOLE BOW FOR THE CROTCHETS AND HALF BOW FOR THE
QUAVERS.

NOTE TO THE ADVANCED PLAYER

See A NEW APPROACH TO VIOLIN PLAYING (pp.46, 47), that is how
double-stops should be practised in the scales.

LESSON XII

EIGHT SONGS FOR TWO VIOLINS

Let us have a grand summary before ending the course with the twelfth lesson.

PLEASE NEVER FORGET

(a) That the violin is a work of art, and should be treated as such.

(b) That the core of all violin playing is in a beautiful tone; because only through a quality of tone, which has the power to move, can one find a true artistic outlet. And this entirely depends on the correct use of the fundamental balances.

(c) That violin playing through this Approach is like a chain of links; each point of balance is interlocked with and interdependent of another, to create an effortless power of strength.

(d) That no physical action can take place without an order from the mind; and that if the mind is disciplined to give orders only to those basic points which are the key positions of the fundamental balances, these in turn will have the power to motivate a chain of other actions as well.

(e) That the delicate interval colouring is closely connected with ear training, with the preparation of each note and the continuous shift of balances in the left hand finger action.

And now, because of the close resemblance of violin playing to singing, I have decided to end the course with the twelfth lesson in the form of a Grande Finale, with eight folk songs arranged for two violins. Each part is playable by the pupil.

I tried to choose familiar tunes, and they are all great favourites of mine.

Please sing them first, and then play them alone, slowly, checking on all the points of balance. Only then play them together.

But then please try to get (and give!) as much enjoyment out of them as possible, for making music should always be a form of celebration.

And if you have half the pleasure of learning to make music with the violin as I have had in teaching it, this book will have succeeded in its aim.

SWEET BETSY FROM PIKE

SHENANDOAH

THE FOGGY FOGGY DEW

LINCOLNSHIRE POACHER

THERE WAS AN OLD WOMAN

LOCH LOMOND

BARBARA ALLEN

EARLY ONE MORNING

STAGE FRIGHT

ITS CAUSES AND CURES

WITH SPECIAL REFERENCE TO VIOLIN PLAYING

BY

KATO HAVAS

=== CONTENTS ===

also by Kato Havas
A NEW APPROACH TO VIOLIN PLAYING
THE TWELVE LESSON COURSE